thread & bobbin

by alison newman & kait witte

acknowledgements and dedication

This book is dedicated with love to the memory of Darren Newman.

We wish to thank:

Carol Newman and the team at All American Crafts who made this entire project possible.

Charles Witte for bringing his matchless eye to the photos for the book.

Sue Harvey, our fearless editor.

Our parents, who taught us to respect hard work, appreciate the past, and value family and friends.

Our grandmothers, who we hope to emulate in spirit as well as craft.

Steve and Clover for their patience and support.

Ken Hurd for his guidance and hard work throughout the creative process.

We also wish to acknowledge the following for their contributions, both large and small:

Alyna, Thomas, and Olive Witte
Kate Porter
Doreen and Ellie Feuster
Laurette Koserowski
Janome America, Inc.
Pam Mostek
Randy Thomas
Hillary Garris and Can Dalokay
Katie Clements
Liz Johnson and Sew4home.com
Kathy Miller and Michael Miller Fabrics

thread & bobbin

Published by
All American Crafts Publishing, Inc.

All American Crafts, Inc.
7 Waterloo Road
Stanhope, NJ 07874
www.allamericancrafts.com

Publisher | **Jerry Cohen**

Chief Executive Officer | **Darren Cohen**

Product Development Director | **Brett Cohen**

Editor | **Sue Harvey**

Art Director | **Kelly Albertson**

Photography | **Charles Witte and Van Zandbergen Photography**

Product Development Manager | **Pamela Mostek**

Vice President/Quilting Advertising & Marketing | **Carol Newman**

Every effort has been made to ensure that the information presented is accurate. Since we have no control over physical conditions, individual skills, or chosen tools and products, the publisher disclaims any liability for injuries, losses, untoward results, or any other damages which may result from the use of the information in this book. Thoroughly read the instructions for all products used to complete the projects in this book, paying particular attention to all cautions and warnings shown for that product to ensure their proper and safe use.

No one forgets the day they meet their college roommate for the first time. Blank walls and regulation furniture set the backdrop for parents bustling in and out. We hang our posters, put our favorite books on shelves, and drape our grandmothers' quilts over the foot of the beds to make things feel more like home. When we smile and shake our roommate's hand for the first time, we ask ourselves, "Will this person be the kind of friend who becomes like a sister?" Well, for a lucky few, our first year roommate turns out to be just that.

Like many freshman roommates, we were an unlikely pair; but unlikely pairs often make the best of friends. We cemented our connection over hundreds of nights of talking in our first college dorm room, and found that our interests overlapped—from music to sewing.

Our professional collaboration began when Alison started working for a company that offered craft project tutorials. She immediately thought of Kait, who had spent the previous few years developing and making her own line of handbags. Soon after, we developed an Etsy site to sell some of our crafts. When the opportunity presented itself for us to create a book together, it felt like the perfect culmination of many years of working together.

The nature of crafting is collaborative: for hundreds of years, women would gather around a quilt, pouring their energy into creating something beautiful, all the while deepening their relationships by talking about their lives and sharing each others' company. Crafting is also something that you can share with others through giving, not just creating. We all get tremendous pleasure from the gesture of presenting someone we love with a gift that we have made with our own hands. For the two of us, this pleasure, this desire to create and to give, comes from our grandmothers, both of whom were gifted craftswomen. Their talent and love for sewing has been passed through our mothers and aunts to us, and we honor their gift in this book.

Beyond the act of crafting, of course, are the objects it produces: treasured quilts, afghans, Halloween costumes, wedding veils. These precious, homemade items are the objects in our lives that have the most meaning. We have already been able to pass to our children, nieces and nephews the items that our grandmothers sewed for us as girls. We, in turn, have created clothes and quilts and name blocks for these precious new babies. One day they'll pack these objects into boxes and take them to a new place, and with them their new spaces will feel like home.

This book, of course, is also a craft—a project we've built by hand to pass on to you. We created each of the projects as something that can easily be given as a gift, yet has everyday utility. To us, the point of crafting is to create a lifestyle in which handmade items can be easily made, and then treasured and enjoyed. We hope that the act of creating these projects is as much a gift as the objects themselves will be.

contents

hostess apron

Finished Size: Approximately 21″ x 34″
Finished Block Size: 10″
Skill Level: Intermediate

Fabric

• 1 yard retro print
• 1 yard light green polka dot
• Fat quarter dark turquoise solid
• Fat quarter pale turquoise solid

Supplies & Notions

• Thread in color to match fabrics
• 1/4 yard 44″-wide iron-on interfacing
• 2 1/2 yards trim (optional)
• Basic sewing supplies

Cutting

From the retro print:
One 21 1/2″ x 35″ piece (for skirt)
Two 3″ x 36″ strips (for waist ties)

From the light green polka dot:
One 5″ x 42″ strip; recut into one 5″ x
    20″ piece (for waistband) and four
    5″ C squares (for String Bean
    blocks)
One 5″ x 35″ strip (for skirt facing)
Two 3″ x 36″ strips (for waist tie lining)
Two 10 1/2″ squares (for pocket lining)

This **sweet apron** is perfect
for everyday cooking.

From the dark turquoise solid:
One 10⁷/₈" square; recut in half on the diagonal to make two A triangles
(for String Bean blocks)

From the pale turquoise solid:
One 10⁷/₈" square; recut in half on the diagonal to make two B triangles
(for String Bean blocks)

From the iron-on interfacing:
One 5" x 20" piece (for waistband)

Building Blocks

Make the String Bean Blocks
Note: Use a ¼" seam allowance to stitch blocks.

1. Stitch an A triangle to a B triangle on the long side. Open and press seam toward the A triangle.

2. Draw a diagonal line on the back side of each C square.

3. Place a C square right sides together on the A side of the pieced unit. Stitch on the drawn line. Trim seam allowance to ¼".

4. Press the C corner open.

5. Repeat on the B corner to complete one 10½" x 10½" block.

6. Repeat to make a second block.

Instructions

Note: Use a 1/2" seam allowance throughout unless otherwise noted.

Add Pockets

1. To add optional rickrack, cut lengths to fit along the seams of the String Bean blocks. Pin in place and topstitch along the center of the trim.

2. Place the quilt blocks right sides together with the 10 1/2" light green lining squares. Stitch all around, leaving a 2" opening on one side for turning.

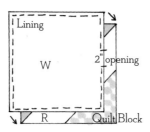

3. Clip the corners and turn right side out through the opening. Press. Turn the opening edges in.

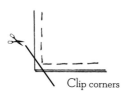

Clip corners

4. Position the pockets on the 21 1/2" x 35" retro skirt piece 4" from one 35" edge and 4" from the 21 1/2" side edges. Pin in place. Stitch the sides and bottom of the pockets, backtacking at the beginning and end of the stitching lines.

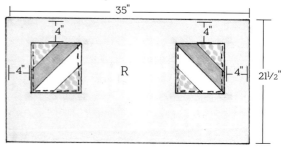

Add Facing to Skirt Bottom

1. To add optional rickrack to the bottom of the apron skirt, cut two 35" lengths. Measure up 1 1/4" from the bottom edge of the skirt and pin a length of rickrack in place. Measure up 2 1/4" from the bottom edge and add another length of rickrack. Stitch in place along the center of the rickrack.

2. Place the light green bottom facing piece right sides together along the bottom edge of the skirt. Pin and stitch in place. Press the seam toward the facing piece.

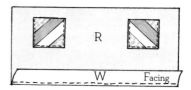

3. Hem the sides of the skirt/facing piece using a ¼" double-turn hem. (See Sewing Basics, page 95.)

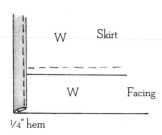

¼" hem

4. Fold the bottom edge of the facing under ¼" and press. Turn the facing to the wrong side of the skirt. Stitch along the edge of the facing.

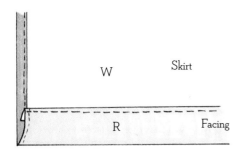

Gathering the Waist

1. Stitch along the top of the skirt piece ⅛" from the edge using a long basting stitch. Do not backtack. Leave 4" thread tails at the beginning and end of the stitching.

2. Sew another line of stitches ¼" from the top edge. Do not back tack and leave 4" thread tails at both ends of stitching.

3. Gently pull the top thread from each line of stitching to gather the edge. Adjust the gathers until they are evenly spaced and the top of the skirt measures 19".

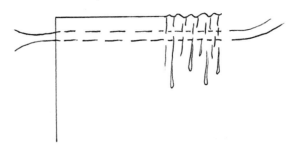

Create the Waist Ties

1. Place the waist tie strips right sides together with the light green waist tie lining strips.

2. Mark a point on one end of the layered strips. Stitch along the long edges of the strips and on the marked lines, leaving the other end open for turning.

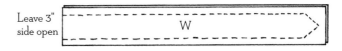

Leave 3" side open

W

allowance. Turn the ties right side out. Press.

4. Topstitch around the outside of the ties.

5. Create a 1¼" pleat on the raw end of each tie. Stay stitch the pleat to hold it in place.

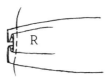

3. Place a waist tie right sides together on each end of the waistband below the center line. Baste in place.

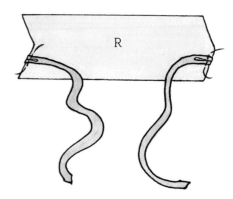

Create the Waistband

1. Adhere the interfacing strip to the wrong side of the light green waistband strip.

2. Fold the waistband strip in half along the length and press to mark the center of the strip.

Sew Waistband to Skirt

1. Stitch the waistband to the edge of the skirt with right sides together. You should have ½" of waistband on either side of the gathers. Press the waistband up away from the skirt.

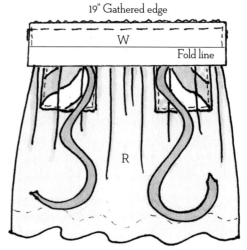

Front View

2. Fold the waistband in half along the long edge with right sides together, sandwiching the ties between the layers.

3. Stitch both ends using a 1/2″ seam allowance. Be sure to stop stitching 1/2″ from the bottom edges. Backtack at the beginning and end of the stitching lines.

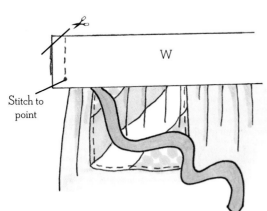

Stitch to point

W

4. Clip the corners and turn the waistband right side out. Press.

5. Fold the bottom edge of the waistband under 1/2″ and pin along the back of the skirt. Slipstitch in place and press. (See Sewing Basics, page 92.)

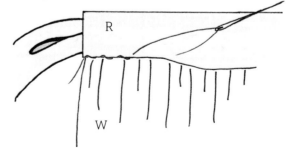

R

W

6. Topstitch 1/8″ from the edge around the waistband.

bib apron

This is an **easy adaptation** of the Hostess Apron with a different quilt block as the pockets. **Mix and match the blocks** throughout this book for a different look, and add trim **as you desire.**

Finished Size: approximately 30" x 35"
Finished Block Size: 9"
Skill Level: Intermediate

Fabric

• 1 yard blue and white floral
• ³/₄ yard red, pink and cream floral
• ³/₄ yard white floral
• ¹/₄ yard red geometric print

Supplies & Notions

• Thread in color to match fabrics
• ¹/₄ yard 20"-wide iron-on interfacing
• Basic sewing supplies

Cutting

From the blue and white floral:
One 21¹/₂" x 35" piece (for skirt)
Two 10¹/₂" x 12" pieces (for bib, bib lining)

From the red, pink and cream floral:
Two 3" x 36" strips (for waist ties)
Two 3" x 20" strips (for waistband)
Two 3" x 28" strips (for neck ties)
Two 5³/₈" squares; recut in half on the diagonal to make four A triangles
 (for Pinwheel blocks)

From the white floral:
One 5" x 35" piece (for skirt facing)
Two 3" x 36" pieces (for waist tie lining)
One 9¹/₂" x 42" strip; recut into two 9¹/₂" squares (for pocket lining) and
 four 5³/₈" squares. Cut each 5³/₈" square in half on the diagonal to make eight
 B triangles (for Pinwheel blocks)

From the red geometric print:
Two 5³/₈" squares; recut in half on the diagonal to make four A triangles
 (for Pinwheel blocks)

From the iron-on interfacing:
Two 3" x 20" pieces (for waistband)

Building Blocks

Make the Pinwheel Blocks

1. Stitch an A triangle to a B triangle on the long side. Open and press seam toward the print/floral triangle. Repeat to make a total of eight triangle units.

2. Sew a print and floral triangle unit together to make a row. Press seam in one direction. Repeat to make a total of four rows. Stitch two rows together to complete one 9¹/₂" x 9¹/₂" block. Press seam in one direction. Repeat to make a second block.

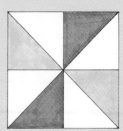

Instructions

Make the Skirt

1. Refer to the following sections for the Hostess Apron on pages 8 and 9 to complete the skirt for this apron: Add Pockets, Add Facing to Skirt Bottom, Gathering the Waist, and Create the Waist Ties.

Create the Bib and Neck Ties

1. Fold each long edge of the neck ties under ½" and press. Fold in half along the length, matching the folded edges. Pin and topstitch along the long sides. Press. Fold one end of each tie under ½". Fold under 1/2" again. Press and stitch to create a small hem.

2. Baste ties at least ³/₄" from the sides on the right side of a blue and white floral bib piece.

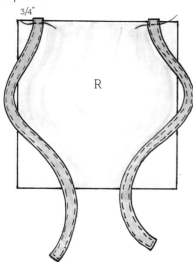

3. Place the bib lining piece right sides together with the tie/bib piece. Stitch together on the sides and top edges, sandwiching the ties between the layers. Clip the corners. Turn right side out and press. Topstitch along the top and both sides.

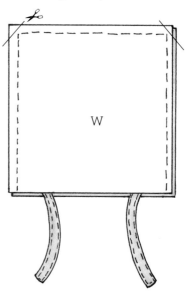

Create the Waistband and Attach the Bib

1. Adhere the interfacing to the wrong side of the floral waistband strips.

2. Center the waist ties right sides together on the short edges of one 3" x 20" waistband piece. Baste in place.

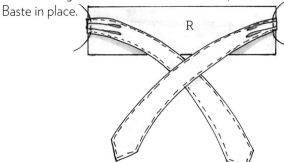

3. Place the remaining waistband strip right side up on your work surface. Place the bottom edge of the bib right side up on the waistband strip. Place the waistband/tie strip right side down on the bib. Pin the layers together.

4. Stitch along one long side of the waistband and both ends, stopping stitching ½" from the bottom edge. Clip corners. Turn the waistband right side out. Press.

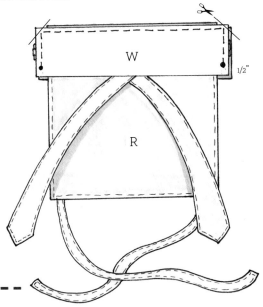

Attach Waistband and Bib to Skirt

1. Stitch one raw edge of the waistband to the gathered edge of the skirt with right sides together, backtacking at both ends. Press the waistband/bib up away from the skirt.

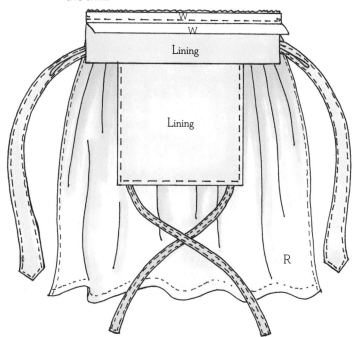

2. Fold the remainig raw edge of the waistband under ½" and pin along the back of the skirt. Slipstitch in place and press.

3. Topstitch ⅛" from the edge around the waistband.

potholders

You can **easily make these potholders** from the **scraps** of another project.

Finished Size: 8″ x 8″
Finished Block Size: 8″
Skill Level: Beginner

Fabric

- Fat eighth orange print
- Fat eighth orange floral
- Fat quarter cream solid
- Fat quarter blue floral
- $3/8$ yard duck canvas

Supplies & Notions

- Thread in colors to match fabrics
- $3/8$ yard heat-resistant batting

Cutting

Note: Cutting and instructions make two identical potholders.

From the orange print:
Two $4^7/8$″ squares; recut in half on the diagonal to make four A triangles
   (for the Pinwheel blocks)

From the orange floral:
Two $4^7/8$″ squares; recut in half on the diagonal to make four A triangles
   (for the Pinwheel blocks)

From the cream solid:
Four $4^7/8$″ squares; recut in half on the diagonal to make eight B triangles
   (for the Pinwheel blocks)

From the blue floral:
Four $8^1/2$″ squares (for the back and pocket)
Two 2″ x 5″ pieces (for hanging loops)

From the duck canvas:
Two $8^1/2$″ squares

From the heat-resistant batting:
Two $8^1/2$″ squares

Make the Pinwheel Blocks

1. Stitch an A triangle to a B triangle on the long side. Open and press seam toward the print/floral triangle. Repeat to make a total of eight triangle units.

2. Sew a print and floral triangle unit together to make a row. Press seam in one direction. Repeat to make a total of four rows. Stitch two rows together to complete one $8^1/2$″ x $8^1/2$″ block. Press seam in one direction. Repeat to make a second block.

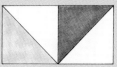

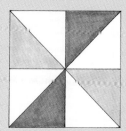

Hint

The pieces used for creating the Pinwheel blocks are triangles. This means that they have one edge cut on the bias, in this case the long edge of the triangle. A bias edge is cut diagonally to the grain of the fabric. This edge is prone to stretching and will distort quilt blocks if handled too much prior to sewing. Be very careful when working with these triangles.

Instructions

Use a $1/4$" seam allowance throughout.

Create the Back Pockets

1. Turn one edge of an $8^{1}/_{2}$" back pocket square under $1/4$" and press. Turn under another $1^{1}/_{4}$" and press to make a double-turn hem. Stitch along the fold of the hem $1/8$" from the inside folded edge. Repeat to make a second hemmed square.

2. Layer a hemmed square right side up on top of an unhemmed back pocket square.

3. Baste the two pieces together on the three unhemmed sides using a $1/8$" seam allowance. Repeat with the second hemmed square and remaining unhemmed square.

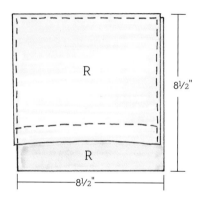

Quilt and Layer the Potholders

1. Layer a Pinwheel block right side up on top of a duck canvas square and place a batting square on the bottom.

2. Pin and baste in place around all edges.

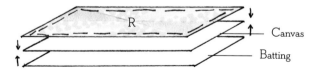

Canvas

Batting

3. Stitch in the ditch of the seams of the quilt block through all layers.

4. Repeat steps 1—3 with the remaining Pinwheel block.

5. Fold the long edges of the 2" x 5" hanging loop pieces under $1/2$" and press. Fold the piece in half along the long edge, matching the folded edges. Press. Topstitch $1/8$" from the edge on both long sides.

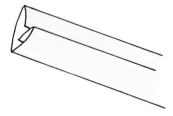

6. Fold a hanging loop in half and pin it in the corner of a quilted panel. Baste in place. Repeat with the second hanging loop and quilted panel.

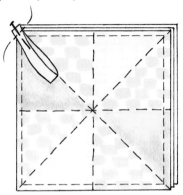

Finish the Potholders

1. Place a back pocket piece right sides together with a quilted panel, sandwiching the hanging loop between the layers. As you position the layers, make sure that when the potholder is turned right side out, the loop will be located in a corner near the opening of the back pocket.

2. Stitch around the edges of the potholder, leaving a 3" opening on one side for turning. Be careful to catch only the raw ends of the hanging loop in the seam.

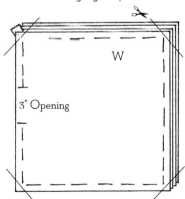

W

3" Opening

3. Clip the corners. Turn right side out through the opening and press. Turn the edges of the opening in and slipstitch closed. (See Sewing Basics on page 92).

4. Topstitch around the outside ¼" from the edge to finish one potholder.

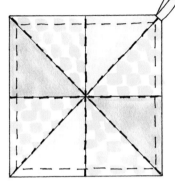

5. Repeat steps 1–4 to complete the second potholder.

kitchen

tea towels

Add a **splash of color** to a functional tea towel with this **easy appliqué design.**
They make a **wonderful housewarming gift,** or make a few using **seasonal fabrics**
and rotate them **throughout the year.**

Finished Size: 17½" x 26"
Skill Level: Beginner

Fabric (makes two)

- 1⅝ yards linen or four premade tea towels with hemmed edges removed
- Scrap orange floral
- Scrap orange print
- ¼ yard lightweight white fabric

Supplies & Notions

- White thread
- Heat transfer pencil
- Embroidery floss (we used olive green)
- Embroidery needle
- 8" embroidery hoop
- Basic sewing supplies

Cutting

From the linen:
Four 18" x 26½" panels (for bases)

From the orange floral scrap:
Two 2" x 6" pieces (for hanging loops)

Cutting Appliqué Pieces
Note: Refer to Faced Appliqué on page 93. Use patterns given on the pull-out pattern sheets to cut pieces.

From the orange floral scrap:
One Vase 1
One Vase 2

From the orange print scrap:
One Vase 2

From the lightweight white fabric:
One Vase 1
Two Vase 2

Instructions

Embroider the Herbs

Note: You will need one Herb A, one Herb B, and one reversed Herb B. The patterns given are used for the tea towel with two motifs. For the herb motif used on the second towel, place the Herb B embroidery design against a window. Trace the design onto the back side of the paper to create the reversed pattern.

1. Trace the embroidery patterns found on the pull-out pattern sheets using a heat transfer pencil. Roughly cut out the patterns. Position Herb A, face down, in the bottom left hand corner of one of the linen base pieces at least 2″ from the left edge and 6¼″ from the bottom edge.

2. Position Herb B, face down, to the right of Herb A at least 7″ from the left edge and 4″ from the bottom edge.

3. Position the reversed Herb B, face down, in the bottom right hand corner of one of the linen base pieces at least 2¼″ from the right edge and 4″ from the bottom edge.

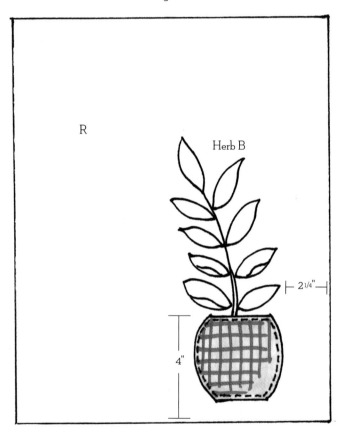

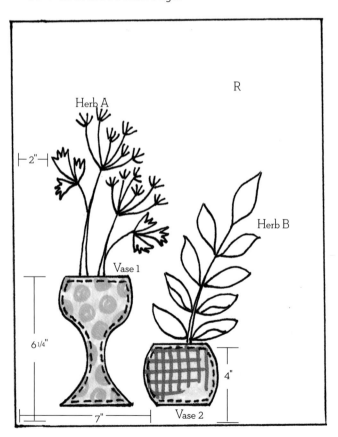

4. Using a hot iron, press the paper patterns until the heat transfers the pencil lines. Remove the patterns.

5. Embroider on the transferred lines using a backstitch (see Hand Embroidery Stitches on page 92.)

Add the Vases

1. Prepare the vases for appliqué according to the Faced Appliqué instructions on page 93.

2. Arrange the vases on the linen bases so it looks like the herbs are coming out of each vase. Pin in place and machine stitch very close to the edge all around using a straight stitch. Backtack at the beginning and end of each stitching line.

Add the Hanging Loops

1. Turn the long sides of each 2″ x 6″ orange floral piece 1/2″ to the wrong side and press. Fold in half along the length with wrong sides together. Press. Stitch on both long sides 1/8″ from the edge.

2. Fold the strips in half to create 3″ loops.

3. Pin the loops in the center of the top right-side edge on the embroidered bases, aligning raw edges. Baste in place.

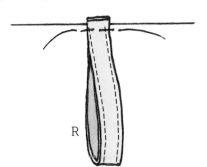

R

Finish the Tea Towels

1. Place an embroidered base and a plain 18″ x 26 1/2″ linen base right sides together. Pin, then stitch around the perimeter using a 1/4″ seam allowance. Leave a 3″ opening in one side for turning.

2. Clip the corners, turn the towel right side out through the 3″ opening and press. Turn the opening edges to the inside. Slipstitch the opening closed. (See Sewing Basics, page 92.)

3. Topstitch around the perimeter of the towel 1/4″ from the edge.

4. Repeat to complete the second towel.

kitchen

chef's apron

Finished Size: 28" x 29"
Skill Level: Beginner

Fabric

- 2 yards beige/brown heavyweight cotton stripe
- 1 yard cream solid

Supplies & Notions

- Thread in colors to match fabric
- Brown embroidery floss
- Embroidery needle
- 8" embroidery hoop
- 32" square craft or wrapping paper
- Heat transfer pencil
- Two 1¼" D-rings
- 1 yard 20"-wide iron-on interfacing
- Pinking shears (optional)
- Basic sewing supplies

Cutting

Note: Fold the craft or wrapping paper in half. Make a pattern for the apron.

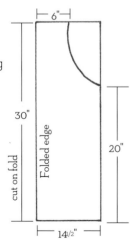

6"

30"

cut on fold

Folded edge

20"

14½"

We put a **masculine touch** on a **simple apron** to create this great Chef's Apron. While **perfect for a barbeque,** the understated embroidery lends itself to more **formal entertaining as well.**

From the beige/brown stripe:
One apron piece with stripe running down the length of the apron
One 38$^{1}/_{2}$″ x 42″ strip; recut two 2$^{1}/_{2}$″ x 38$^{1}/_{2}$″ strips (for waist ties), one 3$^{1}/_{2}$″ x 26″ strip (for neck strap), one 22″ x 25″ piece (for pocket), and one 3″ x 5″ piece (for D-ring tab)

From the cream solid:
One apron piece (for lining)

From the iron-on interfacing:
One 3$^{1}/_{2}$″ x 26″ strip (for neck strap)
One 3″ x 5″ piece (for D-ring tab)

Instructions
Use a $^{1}/_{2}$″ seam allowance throughout.

1. Trace the Whisk and Spoon patterns given on the pull-out pattern sheets onto paper with the heat transfer pencil. Place the traced design face down on the front of the apron. Press for 60 seconds with a hot iron to transfer the design to the apron.

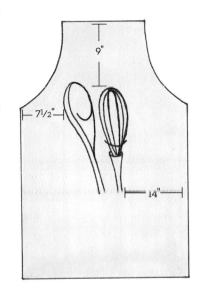

2. Place a section of the design into the embroidery hoop and tighten to make the fabric taut.

3. Use a backstitch to embroider the design. (See Hand Embroidery Stitches in Sewing Basics on page 92.)

4. Move the hoop to a new section and embroider the design. Continue in this way until the design is complete.

Make the Neck Strap, Waist Ties and D-Ring Tab

1. Adhere the interfacing pieces to the wrong side of the neck strap and D-ring tab pieces.

2. Fold the two long edges of the neck strap piece under ½" and press. Fold the strap in half along the length, matching the folded edges. Press. Pin and stitch along the long edges ⅛" from the edge. Fold one short end under ½" and press. Fold the end under another 1". Stitch in place to create a hem.

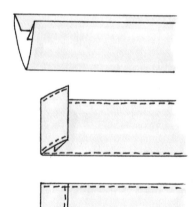

3. Repeat step 2 with the waist ties and D-ring tab, except do not hem the end of the D-ring tab.

4. Slip the tab strip through the two D-rings. Fold the strip in half to form a loop. Baste raw edges together.

5. Baste the raw ends of the neck strap and D-ring loop on the top edge of the apron 1" from the top corners. Baste the raw ends of the waist ties to the side edges of the apron 1" down from the arm curve.

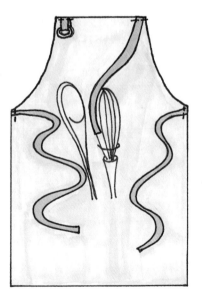

Attach the Lining to the Apron

1. Place the cream solid apron lining piece right sides together with the apron piece, sandwiching the neck strap, D-ring tab and waist ties between the layers. Stitch around the top and side edges, leaving the bottom edge open. Clip the corners and curves. Turn right side out through the bottom. Press.

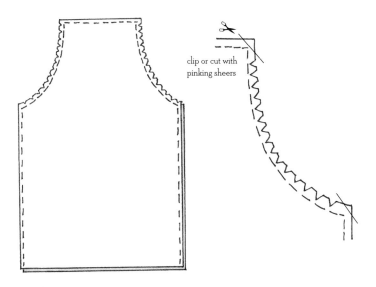

clip or cut with pinking sheers

Hint

Use pinking shears for trimming curved corners to allow for a bit more 'give' in the apron armhole curves. The spaces between the teeth will allow the fabric a small amount of stretch.

2. Turn the bottom edge under 1/2" and press. Turn under another 1" and press. Stitch through all layers to create a hem along the bottom edge.

3. Topstitch around the sides and top of the apron 1/8" from the edge.

Add the Pocket

1. Fold the pocket piece in half with right sides together to make a 12 1/2" x 22" piece.

2. Stitch along the sides and bottom, leaving a 3" opening on one side for turning. Clip the corners and turn right side out through the 3" opening. Turn the opening edges in. Press.

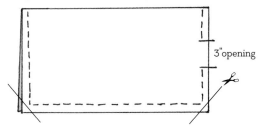

3" opening

3. Position the pocket on the front of the apron, centering it between both edges, positioning the top edge of the pocket to look like the whisk and spoon are in the pocket.

4. Stitch the sides and bottom 1/8" away from the edges. Stitch two vertical lines 7" and 14" in from one side to create three pockets.

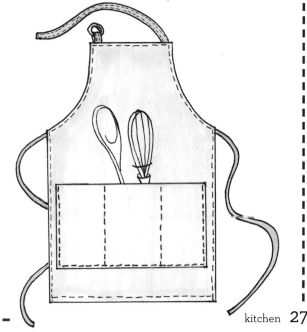

snowball baby blocks

These **baby blocks** are soft and adorable.
Turn them into alphabet blocks using the **appliqué patterns
given** or select certain letters and **spell the name of your
favorite newborn!**

Finished Size: 5″ cube and 2¹/₂″ cube
Finished Block Sizes: 5″ and 2¹/₂″
Skill Level: Intermediate

Fabric
- ¹/₄ yard fabric A
- ¹/₄ yard fabric B
- ¹/₄ yard lining fabric
- Scraps for letters

Supplies & Notions
- Thread in colors to match fabrics
- Scraps of fusible web
- Assorted buttons (if using baby blocks
  for a room decoration only)
- Pointed tool for poking corners
  (knitting needle, chopstick, etc.)
- Embroidery floss and needle
  (for hand appliqué)
- Scrap of tear-away fabric stabilizer
  (for machine appliqué)
- Polyester fiberfill
- Small bell
- Basic sewing supplies

Cutting
Note: The following makes one large
baby block.
From fabric A:
One 5¹/₂″ x 42″ strip; recut into six 5¹/₂″
squares (for A pieces in Snowball
blocks)

From fabric B:
Two 2¹/₂″ x 42″ strips; recut twenty-four
2¹/₂″ squares (for B pieces in Snowball
blocks)

From the lining fabric:
One 5¹/₂″ x 42″ strip; recut into six 5¹/₂″
squares

Instructions
Note: Use a ¹/₄″ seam allowance throughout.

Appliqué the Snowball Blocks
1. Choose the number of blocks that
you will use for appliqué. We included only
one appliquéd Snowball block in each baby
block that we made.

Building Blocks

Make the Snowball Blocks
  1. Draw a diagonal line on the back
side of each B square.
  2. Place a B square right sides together on each corner of an A square.

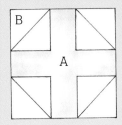

  3. Stitch on the drawn lines. Trim
seam allowances to ¹/₄″. **Note:** To make
the Pinwheel Baby Block, pin each set of
trimmed-off corner triangles together
and save.

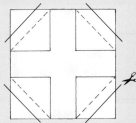

  4. Press the B corners open to make
one 5¹/₂″ x 5 ¹/₂″ block.

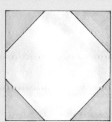

  5. Repeat to make a total of six blocks.

2. Trace the desired letter on the paper side of the fusible web scrap using the patterns given on the pull-out pattern sheets. Cut out the letter, leaving 1/8"–1/4" all around.

3. Fuse the letter to the wrong side of a fabric scrap. Cut out on the drawn lines.

4. Remove the paper backing and fuse the letter to the center of a Snowball block.

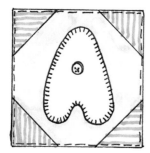

5. Repeat steps 2–4 for each block that you've decided to appliqué.

6. To appliqué by machine, cut a 5 1/2" square of fabric stabilizer. Pin on the wrong side of the center of the Snowball block.

7. Select an appliqué stitch, such as a blanket stitch or a satin stitch.

8. Stitch around the edges of the letter. Refer to Machine Appliqué in Sewing Basics on page 93.

9. When stitching is complete, carefully remove the fabric stabilizer.

10. To appliqué by hand, use a blanket stitch (shown in photo), or backstitch around the edge of each letter. See Hand Embroidery Stitches in Sewing Basics on page 92.

11. When appliqué is complete, add a button accent to represent the opening(s) in a letter, if the baby block will be used as a decoration. Do not add the button if the block will be used as a toy.

Assemble the Baby Block

1. Baste a 51/2" lining square to the wrong side of each Snowball block 1/8" from the edge.

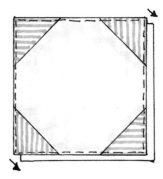

2. With right sides together, stitch four blocks together to make a strip, beginning and ending stitching 1/4" from the corners of the blocks. Backtack at each end of the stitching lines.

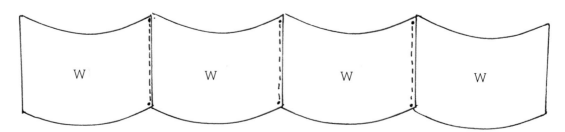

3. Stitch the ends of the strip together in the same way to make a loop.

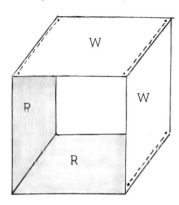

4. Stitch the remaining two blocks into the open spaces to create a box, leaving a 3" opening in one of the seams for turning.

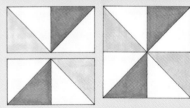

3" Opening

5. Clip corners, and turn right side out through the opening.

6. Use the pointed tool to push out the corners.

7. Half fill the block with polyester fiberfill and add the bell. Add additional fiberfill until the block holds the square shape that you desire.

8. Turn the opening edges in and slipstich the opening closed. (See Sewing Basics, page 92.)

Assemble the Pinwheel Baby Block

1. Cut six 3" squares from the lining fabric.

2. Using the corner triangles trimmed from the Snowball blocks, make six Pinwheel blocks.

3. Refer to Assemble the Baby Block to complete one Pinwheel Baby Block.

Building Blocks

Make the Pinwheel Blocks

1. Stitch two trimmed-off triangles together on the long side. Open and press seam to one side. Repeat to make a total of six triangle units.

2. Trim the triangle units to measure 1³⁄₄" x 1³⁄₄".

3. Sew two triangle units together to make a row. Press seam in one direction. Repeat to make a second row. Stitch the rows together to complete one 3" x 3" block. Press seam in one direction.

4. Repeat to make a total of six blocks.

Note: If using the triangles from only one baby block, reverse placement of the two fabrics in three of the blocks to add interest.

nine-patch play mat

This play mat is the **perfect weekend project.** Use pinks and white as we have to make it girly, or use **bright colors** for a totally different effect. We've seen **fabrics** with a **laminated finish** that would make a great backing **if you plan to use it outside!**

Finished Size: 48" x 48"
Finished Block Size: 9"
Skill Level: Beginner

Fabric

- ¼ yard each of eight coordinating fabrics
- 1²/₃ yards white solid
- 1³/₄ yards backing fabric
- 1 yard coordinating backing fabric

Supplies & Notions

- Twin-size batting (56" x 56" piece)
- Thread in colors to match fabrics
- Basting pins
- Basic sewing supplies

Cutting

From the eight coordinating fabrics:
One 3¹/₂" x 42" strip each fabric; recut sixteen 21" strips (for Nine-Patch block strip sets)
Six 2¹/₂" x 42" strips total; recut twelve 21" strips (for binding)

From the white solid:
One 3¹/₂" x 42" strip; recut two 21" strips (for Nine-Patch block strip sets)
One 18¹/₂" x 18¹/₂" square (for center of Play Mat)
Five 6¹/₂" x 42" strips (for borders)

From the backing fabric:
One 12¹/₂" x length of fabric strip
One 29¹/₂" x length of fabric strip

From coordinating backing fabric:
Two 15¹/₂" x 42" strips (for stripe in backing)

Make the Nine-Patch Blocks

1. Stitch a 3¹/₂" x 21" strip lengthwise between two different 3¹/₂" x 21" strips. Press seams to one side. Repeat to make a total of six strip sets.

2. Crosscut the strip sets into thirty-six 3¹/₂" segments.

3. Choose three different segments. Sew the segments together to create one 9¹/₂" x 9¹/₂" Nine-Patch block. Repeat to make a total of twelve blocks.

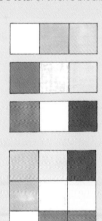

Instructions

Note: Use a ¼" seam allowance throughout.

Create the Play Mat Center

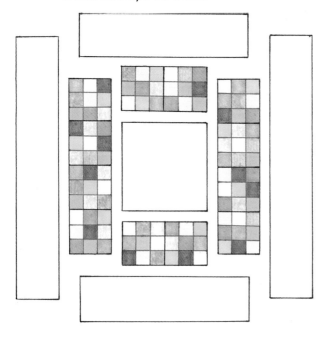

1. Stitch two Nine-Patch blocks together to make a row. Press seam to one side. Repeat to make a second row.

2. Stitch the two rows to the top and bottom of the white 18½" square. Press seams toward the block rows.

3. Stitch four Nine-Patch blocks together to make one row. Press seams to one side. Repeat to make a second row.

4. Stitch the two rows to the remaining sides of the white 18½" square to complete the Play Mat center. Press seams toward the block rows.

Add the Borders

1. Trim two 6½" x 42" white strips to 36½". Pin and stitch these strips to the top and bottom of the Play Mat center. Press seams toward the Play Mat center.

2. Stitch the three remaining 6½" x 42" white strips together on the short ends to make a long strip. Press seams to one side. Cut into two 48½" strips.

3. Stitch the strips to the remaining sides of the Play Mat. Press seams toward the Play Mat center to complete the top.

Create the Backing

1. Stitch the two 15½" x 42" coordinating backing fabric strips short ends together to make one long strip. Trim strip to measure 60".

2. Stitch this strip between the 12½" and 29½" backing fabric strips. Press seams open.

3. Trim backing piece to a 56" square.

Finish the Play Mat

Note: Refer to Quilting in Sewing Basics on page 94 throughout the following steps.

1. Layer the backing face down, then the batting, and the Play Mat top right side up. Baste or pin layers together.

2. Quilt as desired. We quilted diagonal lines through each of the blocks and across the white areas.

3. Remove basting or pins. Trim on all sides.

4. Stitch the twelve 2½" x 21" binding strips short ends together to make one long strip.

5. Attach the binding to the edges of the quilt.

craft apron

Finished Sizes: 17" x 19" (small),
22" x 23" (large)
Skill Level: Beginner

Project Note

Instructions are given for this apron in two sizes—child's sizes small and large. The instructions are written for the small size. Whenever there is a difference in an amount, size, or instruction for the large size, the information immediately follows in red (red).

Fabric

• 2/3 yard (7/8 yard) green floral
• 1/3 yard (1/3 yard) orange polka dot
• 3/4 yard (7/8 yard) green print
• Fabric scraps for appliqué

Supplies & Notions

• Thread in colors to match fabrics
• One 3/4"–1" button
• 1/4 yard 44"–wide iron-on interfacing
• Craft or wrapping paper
• Basic sewing supplies

Whether at craft time, or when **helping in the kitchen, kids get dirty!**
This apron will help to **keep some of the mess off their clothes.**

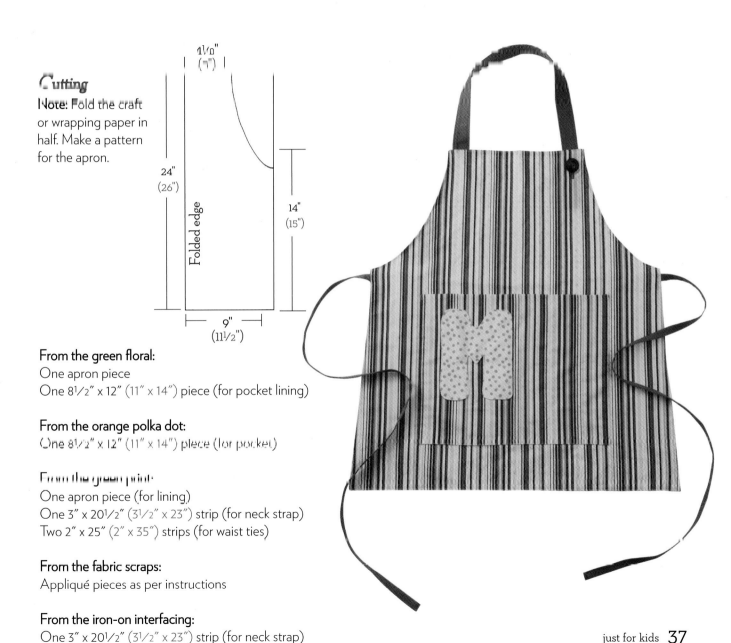

Cutting

Note: Fold the craft or wrapping paper in half. Make a pattern for the apron.

1½"
(¾")

24"
(26")

Folded edge

14"
(15")

9"
(11½")

From the green floral:
One apron piece
One 8½" x 12" (11" x 14") piece (for pocket lining)

From the orange polka dot:
One 8½" x 12" (11" x 14") piece (for pocket)

From the green print:
One apron piece (for lining)
One 3" x 20½" (3½" x 23") strip (for neck strap)
Two 2" x 25" (2" x 35") strips (for waist ties)

From the fabric scraps:
Appliqué pieces as per instructions

From the iron-on interfacing:
One 3" x 20½" (3½" x 23") strip (for neck strap)

Instructions

Use a 1/2" seam allowance throughout.

Make the Pocket

1. Prepare flower, leaf and flower center appliqué pieces referring to Faced Appliqué in Sewing Basics on page 93 and using the patterns given on the pull-out pattern sheets. **Note:** Instead of the flower motif, personalize the apron with the child's initials or first name using the alphabet patterns given on the pull-out pattern sheets.

2. Place the appliqué pieces on the right side of the orange polka dot pocket piece, placing them at least 3/4" from the outer edges of the pocket. Pin and stitch them in place.

3. Place the green floral pocket lining piece right sides together with the appliquéd pocket piece and stitch around the outside, leaving a 2" opening on one side for turning.

4. Clip the corners. Turn right side out through the opening. Turn the opening edges in and press.

5. Place the pocket on the green floral apron piece, centering the top of the pocket 11" (13") above the bottom edge of the apron piece. Stitch the side and bottom 1/8" from the edges, backtacking at the beginning and end of your stitching line.

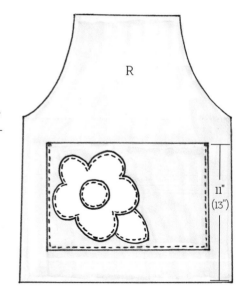

Make the Neck Strap and Waist Ties

1. Apply the interfacing strip to the wrong side of the green print neck strap.

2. Turn the two long edges of the green print neck strap under 1/2" and press. Fold in half along the length, matching the folded edges and press again. Stitch along the long edges 1/8" from the edge. Turn one end under 1/2" and press. Turn under 1/2" again and press. Stitch in place to hem.

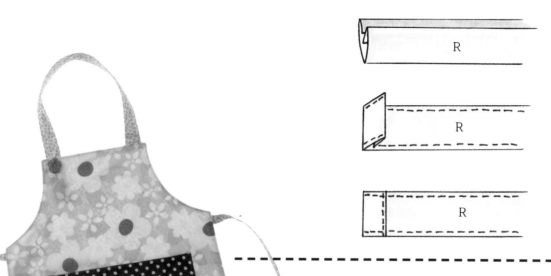

3. Repeat step 2 with the green print waist ties.

4. Baste the unhemmed ends of the neck strap and waist ties to the right side of the apron.

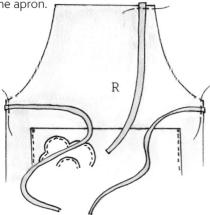

Finish the Apron

1. Place the green print apron lining piece right sides together with the apron piece, sandwiching the neck strap and waist ties between the layers. Stitch around the outside edges, leaving a 5" opening on one side for turning.

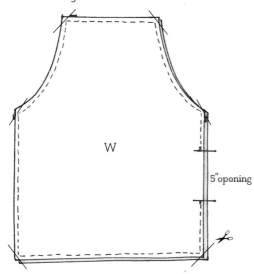

2. Clip the corners and curves. Turn right side out through the opening. Turn the opening edges in and press. Slipstitch the opening closed. Topstitch around the main body of the apron.

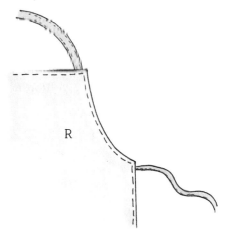

3. Sew the button onto the free end of the neck strap. (See Sewing Buttons in Sewing Basics on page 93.)

4. Mark the buttonhole position on the apron 1½" from the top edge and 1" from the side. Make a buttonhole. (See Making a Buttonhole in Sewing Basics on page 93.)

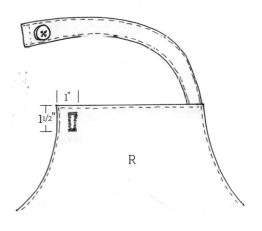

heart tote

Expandable, sweet, and understated, this tote makes a great bag o' tricks for the **busy mom,** or the **perfect accessory** for an afternoon-to-evening trip.

Finished Tote Size: 13" x 16" x 8"
Finished Block Size: 13"
Skill Level: Intermediate

Fabric

- 1 yard tan floral
- 1 1/8 yards beige with brown stripe
- 1 1/4 yards multicolored floral
- 1/2 yard orange polka dot
- 3/4 yard duck canvas (60" wide)

Supplies & Notions

- Thread in colors to match fabrics
- Heavyweight felt 7 1/2" x 12 3/4"
- 1 yard of 20"-wide iron-on interfacing
- One magnetic closure
- One key hook
- Poker for corners (knitting needle, chopstick, etc.)
- Basic sewing supplies

Cutting

From the tan floral:
One 7 1/2" x 42" strip; recut into two 7 1/2" squares (for B piece in Heart block) and four 3 1/2" squares (for A piece in Heart block)
One 9" x 42" strip; recut into two 9" x 17" pieces (for sides)
One 14" x 42" strip; recut into one 14" x 17" piece (for back panel), one 9" x 14" piece (for bottom), and two 2 1/2" x 14" strips (for front panel)

From the beige with brown stripe:
Note: Cut all pieces parallel to the selvage edge.

One 31" x 42" strip; recut into two 5" x 31" strips (for handles), four 4" x 23" strips (for side ties), two 7 1/2" squares (for B piece in Heart block) and four 3 1/2" squares (for A piece in Heart blocks)

From the multicolored floral:
One 14" x 42" strip; recut into two 14" x 17" pieces (for lining front and back)
One 9" x 42" strip; recut into two 9" x 17" pieces (for lining sides)
One 14" x 42" strip; recut into one 9" x 14" piece (for lining bottom), one 12 1/2" x 14" piece (for large inner pocket), and one 6" x 7" piece (for small inner pocket)

Building Blocks

Make the Heart Blocks
Note: Use a 1/2" seam allowance.

1. Draw a diagonal line on the back side of all A and B squares.

2. Place an A square right sides together on two corners of each C piece and a B square on the bottom.

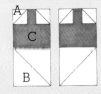

3. Stitch on the drawn lines. Trim seam allowances to 1/4".

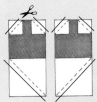

4. Press the A and B corners open.

5. Sew the two halves together, matching the A square seams, to make one 14" x 14" Heart block.

From the orange polka dot:
One 12½″ x 42″ strip; recut into one 12½″ x 14″ piece (for large pocket lining), one 6″ x 7″ piece (for small pocket lining), and one 3″ x 4″ piece (for key hook tab)

From the duck canvas:
One 14″ x 60″ strip; recut into two 14″ x 17″ pieces (for front and back stabilizer)
One 9″ x 60″ strip; recut into two 9″ x 17″ pieces (for side stabilizer) and one 9″ x 14″ piece (for bottom stabilizer)

From the iron-on interfacing:
Two 5″ x 31″ strips (for handles)

Instructions

Note: Use a ½″ seam allowance throughout.

Make the Handles and the Side Ties

1. Apply iron-on interfacing to the wrong side of the 5″ x 31″ stripe handle strips.

2. Fold the handle strips under ½″ on the two long edges and press. Fold in half along the length with wrong sides together, matching the folded edges. Pin and stitch along both long sides ⅛″ from the edge.

3. Fold the 4″ x 23″ stripe tie pieces in half along the length with right sides together. Pin and stitch ½″ from the edge along the long side and one short end. Clip corners, turn right side out, and press. Be sure to poke out the corners so you have crisp right angles.

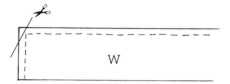

Finish the Outer Shell

1. Stitch the 2½" x 14" tan floral strips to the top and bottom of the Heart block to complete the front panel. Press seams open.

2. Place the front panel and the tan floral back and side pieces wrong side down on the same-size duck canvas pieces. Baste ¼" around the outside edges. Layer the bottom duck canvas piece between the heavyweight felt piece and the tan floral bottom piece. Baste 1/4" around the outside edges.

3. Baste the ties to the right side edges of the front and back panels, 2" down from the top corners. Baste the handles to the right side top edges of the front and back panels 2" in from the corners.

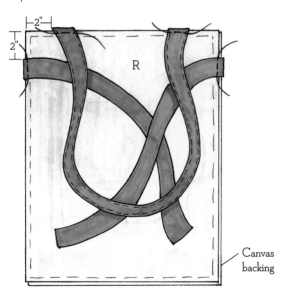

Canvas backing

4. Stitch the bottom edge of the front and back panels to the bottom panel, starting and stopping the stitching ½" from each corner. Backtack at the start and finish of each stitching line.

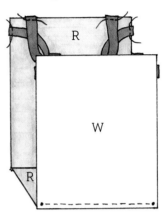

5. Stitch the side panels to the front, back, and bottom pieces with right sides together, starting and stopping stitching ½" from the bottom corners only. Clip bottom corners.

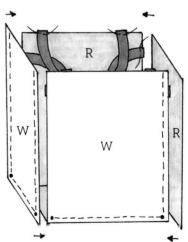

Build the Lining

1. Fold the 3″ x 4″ orange key hook piece under 1/2″ on both long edges and press. Fold in half along the long edge, matching the folded edges. Stitch along both long sides 1/8″ from the edge. Slide the key hook onto the strip and fold the strip in half. Baste the raw ends together.

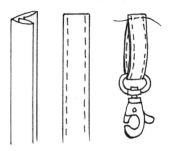

2. Baste the key hook piece to the right side of the 6″ x 7″ multicolored floral piece 2″ in from one corner on a 6″ edge.

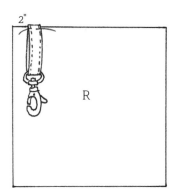

3. Stitch the multicolored floral and orange small pocket pieces with right sides together, sandwiching the key hook tab between the layers. Leave a 2″ opening in one side. Clip the corners, turn right side out through the opening. Turn the opening edges in and press.

4. Stitch the pocket to the right side of one 14″ x 17″ orange lining piece, placing it 2″ from the side and 4″ from the top edge.

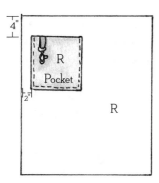

5. Place the 12½″ x 14″ multicolored floral and orange large pocket pieces right sides together. Stitch across one 14″ edge. Turn right side out and press.

6. Place the large pocket on top of the remaining 14″ x 17″ orange lining piece, matching the side and bottom raw edges. Pin and baste around the raw edges.

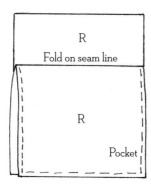

7. Insert a magnetic closure in the top center of the lining pieces 2″ down from the top edge. Follow the manufacturer's instructions and our tips for inserting a magnetic closure on page 94.

8. Assemble the lining referring to steps 4 and 5 of Finish the Outer Shell, leaving a 5″ opening in one side edge for turning.

Finish the Tote

1. Turn the lining right side out and the outer shell wrong side out. Tuck the lining inside the outer shell, right sides together. Match the side seams and the top edges. Pin around the top. Stitch around the top ½″ from the edge.

2. Turn the bag right side out through the opening in the lining, push out the corners and press the top edge.

3. Slipstitch the 5″ opening closed.

4. Topstitch around the top edge of the bag ⅛″ from the edge.

5. Tie the side ties in a bow to complete the tote.

retro handbag

This cute bag is great for **everyday use**—and so versatile. **Just one pair of handles** accommodates a bag for any occasion. The convertible design **makes it easy to switch** from one style or color to another. **The possibilities are endless!** We embellished our bags with purchased trim and our **adorable Fabric Flower** (see instructions on page 82).

Finished Bag Size: Approximately 12″ x 18″
Skill Level: Intermediate

Fabric

- ¾ yard bag fabric
- 1 yard lining fabric
- ¾ yard duck canvas

Supplies & Notions

- Thread to match fabric and trims
- Two 14″-long wooden handles with
  11¼″ openings
- Fourteen ¾″ buttons to coordinate
  with lining
- 15″ x 21″ piece of craft or wrapping paper
- Pointed tool for turning corners
  (knitting needle, chopstick, etc.)
- 7″ zipper to coordinate with lining and
  zipper foot (optional)
- 1¼ yards trim (optional)
- Basic sewing supplies

Cutting

Note: Fold the 15″ x 21″ piece of paper
in half to make a 15″ x 10½″ piece.
Make a pattern for the bag.

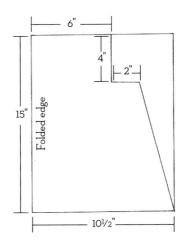

From the bag fabric:
Two bag pieces using paper
    pattern (for outer shell)

From the lining fabric:
Two bag pieces using paper
    pattern
Two 7½" x 10" pieces
    (for optional pocket)

From the duck canvas:
Two bag pieces using paper
    pattern

Instructions
Use a ½" seam allowance throughout.

Build the Outer Shell

1. Baste the duck canvas pieces to
the wrong side of the outer shell
pieces, stitching as close to the edges
as possible.

2. To add optional trim, cut two 20"
lengths. Stitch trim in place on each
outer shell piece at least 2½" above
the bottom edge. Trim even with the
edges of the outer shell pieces.

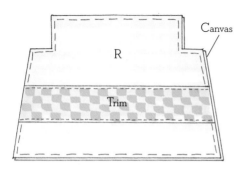

3. Place the outer shell pieces right sides together and stitch along the side and bottom edges. Backtack at the beginning and end of your stitching line. Clip corners.

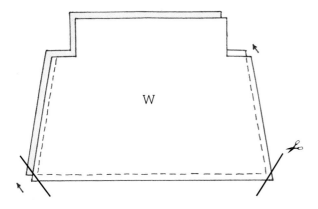

4. Lay the shell on its side, matching the side seam to the bottom seam. This will create a point. Measure 2½" up from the point along the centered side seam and draw a perpendicular line. Stitch along this line backtacking at both ends. Clip the excess fabric leaving a ½" seam allowance. Repeat on the remaining bottom corner. Do not turn right side out.

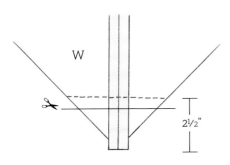

Add the Optional Zipper Pocket

1. Draw a ¼" x 7" rectangle 1¾" down from one 10" edge on the wrong side of a 7½" x 10" pocket piece. Center the marked pocket piece right sides together on one bag lining piece. Pin in place. Stitch around the marked rectangle.

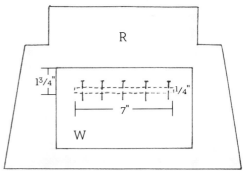

2. Make a slit in the center of the stitched rectangle with small scissors and clip into the corners.

3. Turn the pocket piece right side out through the slit. Press.

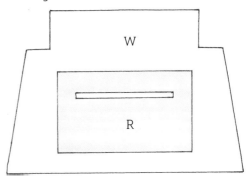

4. Place the zipper face down over the rectangular opening. Pin and then baste in place.

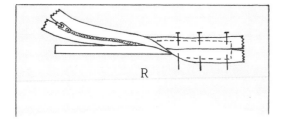

5. Attach the zipper foot to your machine. Stitch around the zipper. Backtack at the beginning and end of your stitching line. Be careful not to stitch over the metal crimper or the metal zipper head at each end of the zipper.

6. Change back to your regular sewing machine foot.

7. Place the remaining 7¹/₂" x 10" pocket piece right sides together with the zipper/pocket piece. Pin in place and stitch around the outside edges, backtacking at the beginning and end of the stitching.

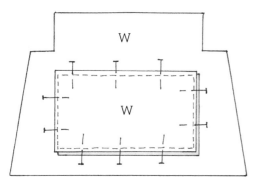

Complete the Lined Shell

1. Place the lining pieces right sides together and stitch along the side and bottom edges, leaving a 4" opening in one side edge for turning. Repeat step 4 of Build the Outer Shell to make box corners. Turn the lining right side out.

2. Tuck the lining inside the outer shell with right sides together, matching side seams and top edges. Pin in place. Stitch around the top edge.

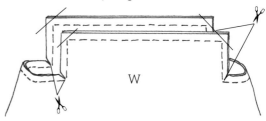

3. Clip corners and turn the bag through the opening in the lining. Poke out all of the corners with a pointed tool.

4. Press the top edge and slipstitch the opening in the lining closed.

Add the Buttons

1. Measure in 1" from each end on the front of each top flap and make a mark 1³/₄" down. Make five more marks spaced 1¹/₂" apart to mark positions for seven buttonholes on each flap.

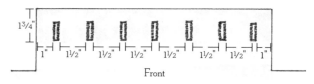

2. Stitch buttonholes to fit ³/₄" buttons according to your sewing machine manual. (See Making a Buttonhole in Sewing Basics on page 93.)

3. Use a seam ripper or small scissors to cut the fabric in the center of your buttonholes, being careful not to cut through the buttonhole end stitches.

4. Turn the bag so the lining is on the outside.

5. Measure down 4¹/₂" on the lining side of the top flaps, directly below each buttonhole and make a mark.

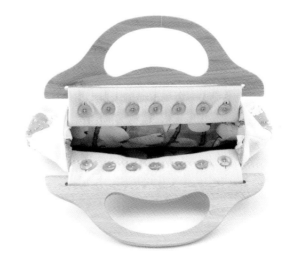

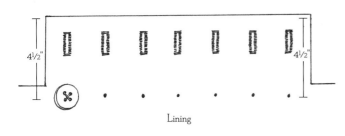

Lining

6. Sew a button at each mark, catching the lining and duck canvas layers only. Do not stitch through the outer shell. (See Sewing Buttons in Sewing Basics on page 93.)

7. Turn the bag right side out, slide the flaps through the wooden handles and button up!

nautical tote

Finished Tote Size: 18″ x 18″
Skill Level: Intermediate

Fabric

• ²⁄₃ yard red, white, and blue plaid
• ¹⁄₄ yard navy and white stripe
• ³⁄₈ yard navy and white floral
• ⁵⁄₈ yard red floral
• ²⁄₃ yard duck canvas (60″ wide)

Supplies & Notions

• One magnetic closure
• Two 1¹⁄₂″ squares of felt or canvas
• Eight grommets with ⁵⁄₈″ inner
  diameter
• Size 5 (⁵⁄₈″) grommet setter
• 2 yards ¹⁄₂″ diameter rope or cord
• Basic sewing supplies

Cutting

From the red, white, and blue plaid:
One 19″ x 42″ strip; recut into two
    6″ x 19″ strips (for A stripe), two
    5″ x 19″ strips (for facing), one
    10″ x 19″ piece (for inner pocket)

From the navy and white stripe:
One 6″ x 42″ strip; recut into two
    6″ x 19″ strips (for B stripe)

Nothing says "Boating" better than blue-toned stripes and rope! This tote is perfect for sunscreen, a good book, a towel, and anything else you need for a day on the water.

From the navy and white floral:
One 9" x 42" strip; recut into two 9" x 19" strips (for C stripe)

From the red floral:
One 15" x 42" strip; recut into two 15" x 19" strips (for lining)

From the duck canvas:
One 19" x 60" strip; recut into two 19" squares

Instructions

Use a 1/2" seam allowance throughout.

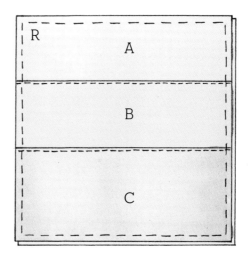

Build the Outer Shell

1. Stitch A, B, and C strips together to build the front and back panels. Press seams toward the C stripe.

2. Place the front panel right side up on a 19" duck canvas square. Stitch around the outside 1/4" from the edge. Topstitch 1/8" below each seam line. Repeat with the back panel.

3. With right sides together and matching the stripes, stitch the front and back panels together on the sides and bottom. Press the side seams open.

4. To create the flat bottom, lay the shell on its side, matching the side seam to the bottom seam. This will create a point. Measure 3¹/₂" up from the point along the center side seam and draw a perpendicular line. Stitch along this line, backtacking at both ends. Clip the excess fabric leaving a ¹/₂" seam allowance. Repeat on the other side seam.

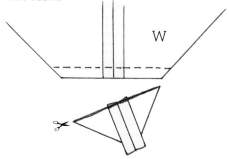

Create the Lining and Add the Pocket

1. Place the 5" x 19" plaid facing pieces right sides together with the 15" x 19" red floral lining pieces, matching along the 19" sides. Pin together and stitch along the 19" side. Press seam down.

2. Fold the 10" x 19" plaid pocket piece in half across the 10" width with right sides together and stitch the sides and bottom leaving a 3" opening on one side. Clip the corners and turn right side out through the opening. Turn the opening edges in. Press.

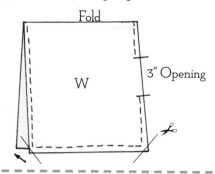

3. Align the folded edge of the pocket piece with the bottom of the facing on one side of the lining, centering the pocket. Stitch the sides and bottom of the pocket, backtacking at the start and finish of the stitching line.

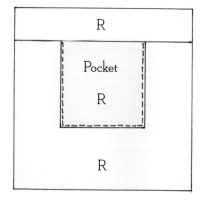

4. Stitch the front and back lining panels together following steps 3 and 4 for Build the Outer Shell. Leave a 5" opening on one side for turning.

Add the Magnetic Closure

1. Measure 2" down from the top edge in the center of the facing pieces and make a mark.

2. Install the magnetic closure at the center marks, following the manufacturer's instructions or referring to Installing a Magnetic Closure on page 94.

Attach the Lining to the Outer Shell

1. Turn the faced lining right side out and the outer shell wrong side out. Tuck the lining inside the outer shell with right sides together. Match the side seams and the top edges. Pin around the top and stitch ½" from the edge.

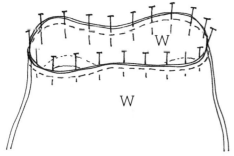

2. Turn the tote right sides out through the opening in the lining, push out the corners and press the top edge.

3. Slipstitch the opening closed.

4. Stitch around the top edge of the tote ⅛" from the edge.

Add Grommets and Rope Handles

1. Mark grommet positions on the outside of the tote 2" and 5" in from each side seam and 1½" down from the top edge.

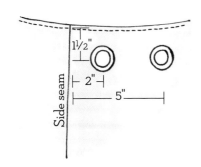

2. Using the grommet setter and following the manufacturer's instructions, insert eight grommets at the marked positions.

3. Cut two 36" lengths of rope. Tie a knot at one end of each length.
Note: Before cutting the rope, wrap a piece of masking tape around it right where you need to cut. Cut through the tape so the ends don't fray. After the rope handles are inserted and tied off, remove the tape.

4. Insert the unknotted end of the rope through the first grommet on the tote front into the inside of the tote. Weave through the rest of the grommets on the front and tie a knot at the remaining end of the rope. Repeat on the back of the tote.
Note: Before tying the knot, make sure the handle length is good. If you'd like shorter handles, just tie the knot higher up and cut off the excess.

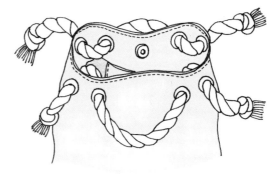

Hint

To make the floral tote, eliminate the plaid and navy-and-white stripe from the Fabric and Cutting lists. Change the navy and white floral and the red floral to ⅔ yard each.

Cut one 19" x 42" strip of navy and white floral; recut into two 15" x 19" pieces (for outer shell), and two 5" x 19" strips (for facing). Cut one 19" x 42" strip of red floral; recut into two 15" x 19" pieces (for lining), and one 10" x 19" piece (for inner pocket). Cut duck canvas as indicated in Cutting.

Ignore step 1 of Build the Outer Shell and use the two 15" x 19" pieces of navy and white floral to make the outer shell.

heart quilt

This is the **perfect quilt** for the **sweetheart in your life.** All of the fabrics in the heart border give it **great possibilities—** **use up your scraps** for lots of color, or stick to a tonal range and **showcase different patterns and textures.**

Finished Quilt Size: 69″ x 87″
Finished Block Sizes: 6″ and 16″
Skill Level: Intermediate

Fabric

- 10 coordinating print fat quarters for Heart blocks
- 2¹⁄₂ yards white solid
- ³⁄₈ yard pink dot
- ¹⁄₂ yard pink mottled
- ³⁄₄ yard pink print
- 2¹⁄₄ yards plaid
- 5¹⁄₂ yards backing

Supplies & Notions

- Double-size batting (77″ x 95″ piece)
- Thread in colors to match fabrics
- Basting pins
- Basic sewing supplies

Cutting

From the fat quarters:
One 8¹⁄₂″ x 16¹⁄₂″ piece from six fat quarters (for piece C in center Heart blocks)
Forty-two sets of two 3¹⁄₂″ x 6¹⁄₂″ pieces (for piece C in border Heart blocks)

From the white solid:
Seven 3¹⁄₂″ x 42″ strips; recut into eighty-four 3¹⁄₂″ squares (for piece B in the border Heart blocks)
Eight 1¹⁄₂″ x 42″ strips; recut into one hundred sixty-eight 1¹⁄₂″ squares (for piece A in the border Heart blocks)
Two 8¹⁄₂″ x 42″ strips; recut into six 8¹⁄₂″ squares (for piece B in the center Heart blocks)
One 3¹⁄₂″ x 42″ strip; recut into twelve 3¹⁄₂″ squares (for piece A in the center Heart blocks)
Two 4″ x 32¹⁄₂″ strips (for center)
One 16¹⁄₂″ x 42″ strip; recut into two 8¹⁄₂″ x 16¹⁄₂″ pieces and two 11¹⁄₂″ x 16¹⁄₂″ pieces (for center)

From the pink dot:
Five 2″ x 42″ strips (for first border)

From the pink mottled:
Six 2″ x 42″ strips (for third border)

From the pink print:
Eight 2¹⁄₂″ x 42″ strips (for binding)

From the plaid:
Six 8¹⁄₂″ x 42″ strips (for second border)
Eight 2″ x 42″ strips (for outer border)
One 6¹⁄₂″ x 42″ strip; recut into four 6¹⁄₂″ squares (for cornerstones)

Building Blocks

Make the Heart Blocks
Note: Use a ¹⁄₂″ seam allowance.

1. Draw a diagonal line on the back side of all 3¹⁄₂″ A and 8¹⁄₂″ B squares.

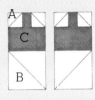

2. Place an A square right sides together on two corners of each 8¹⁄₂″ x 16¹⁄₂″ C piece and a B square on the bottom.

3. Stitch on the drawn lines. Trim seam allowances to ¹⁄₄″.

4. Press the A and B corners open.

5. Sew the two halves together, matching the A square seams, to make one 16¹⁄₂″ x 16¹⁄₂″ center Heart block.

6. Repeat with the 1¹⁄₂″ A squares, 3¹⁄₂″ B squares and 3¹⁄₂″ x 6¹⁄₂″ C pieces to make forty-two 6¹⁄₂″ x 6¹⁄₂″ border Heart blocks.

Note: Save the trimmed-off triangles from the B corners of the border blocks to make the matching pillow sham on page 61.

Instructions

Note: Use a 1/4" seam allowance throughout.

Create the Quilt Center

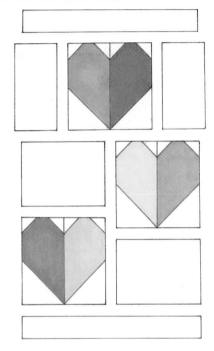

1. Stitch a center Heart block between two 8 1/2" x 16 1/2" white pieces to complete section 1. Press seams toward the white pieces.

2. Stitch an 11 1/2" x 16 1/2" white piece to the top of one center Heart block to complete section 2. Press seam toward the white piece.

3. Stitch the remaining 11 1/2" x 16 1/2" white piece to the bottom of the remaining center Heart block to complete section 3. Press seam toward the white piece.

4. Sew section 2 to section 3. Press seam to one side. Sew section 1 to the top. Press seam toward section 1.

5. Add a 4" x 32 1/2" white strip to the top and bottom to create the quilt center. Press seams toward the white strips.

Add the Borders

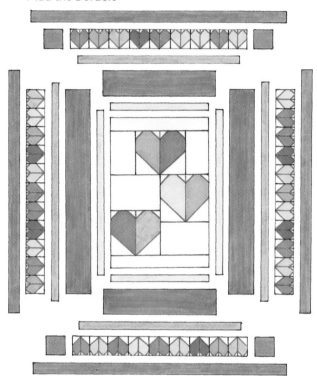

1. Trim two 2" x 42" pink dot strips to 32 1/2". Pin and stitch these strips to the top and bottom of the quilt center. Press seams toward the strips. Stitch the remaining 2" x 42" pink dot strips together on the short ends to make a long strip. Press seams to one side. Cut into two 53 1/2" strips. Stitch these strips to the long sides. Press seams toward the strips.

2. Trim two 8¹/₂" x 42" plaid strips to 35¹/₂". Pin and stitch these strips to the top and bottom of the quilt center. Press seams toward the strips. Stitch the remaining 8¹/₂" x 42" plaid strips together on the short ends to make a long strip. Press seams to one side. Cut into two 69¹/₂" strips. Sew these strips to the long sides. Press seams toward the strips.

3. Stitch the 2" x 42" pink mottled strips together on the short ends to make a long strip. Press seams to one side. Cut into two 51¹/₂" strips and two 72¹/₂" strips. Sew the shorter strips to the top and bottom and the longer strips to the long sides of the quilt center. Press seams toward the strips.

4. Sew 12 border Heart blocks together to create a border strip. Press seams to one side. Repeat to make a second border strip. Pin and stitch the strips to the sides of the quilt center. Press seams toward the pink mottled border.

5. Sew nine heart blocks together to create a border strip. Press seams to one side. Add a 6¹/₂" plaid cornerstone to each end to complete one quilt border. Press seams toward the cornerstones. Repeat to create a second border. Pin and stitch these borders to the top and bottom of the quilt center. Press seams toward the pink mottled border.

6. Stitch the 2" x 42" plaid strips together on the short ends to make a long strip. Press seams to one side. Cut into two 66¹/₂" strips and two 87¹/₂" strips. Sew the shorter strips to the top and bottom and the longer strips to the long sides of the quilt center. Press seams toward the strips to complete the top.

Hint

If you will be using the quilt on a bed, turn the side and bottom Heart borders to place the tops of the hearts against the quilt center. The hearts will be right side up as they hang over the edge of the bed.

Or, turn every other block when joining them to make the border strips as shown. The quilt will look great wherever it's used!

Stitching pieced borders can be difficult—especially if your piecing is off, even by small increments. It is best to use lots of pins when adding the border, and work in "halves." Fold the quilt top in half across the center and crease to mark the center of each long side. Place a border strip right sides together along the edge of the quilt center. Match up the end of the border strip with the edge of the quilt center and pin in place. Do the same with the other end of the border strip. Now, find the center of the pieced border (six quilt blocks in from either end) and pin it to the creased center of the quilt edge. Evenly pin the border strip between the center and ends to the edge of the quilt center.

Finish the Quilt

Note: Refer to Quilting in Sewing Basics on page 94 throughout the following steps.

1. Prepare a 77" x 95" backing piece.

2. Layer the backing right side down, then the batting and quilt top right side up. Baste or pin layers together.

3. Quilt as desired. Remove pins or basting. Trim on all sides.

4. Stitch the eight 2½" x 42" binding strips short ends together to make one long strip.

5. Attach the binding to the edges of the quilt.

pinwheel pillow sham

Start with new fabrics to make this pillow sham or use the scraps left over from the Heart Quilt.

Finished Sham Size: 26" x 20"
Finished Block Size: 5"
Skill Level: Beginner

Fabric

- Large scrap of 8 different prints or trimmed-off triangles from the Heart Quilt
- ⅓ yard white solid or trimmed-off triangles from the Heart Quilt
- ⅜ yard plaid
- ⅔ yard backing fabric
- ⅔ yard light-color lining fabric

Supplies & Notions

- Thread in color to match fabrics
- Standard pillow
- Basic sewing supplies

Cutting

Note: If using trimmed-off triangles from the Heart Quilt, disregard cutting for the print scraps and white solid.

From each print scrap:
Two 3⅜" squares. Cut each square in half diagonally to make four triangles of each fabric. (for Pinwheel blocks)

From the white solid:
Two 3⅜" x 42" strips; recut into sixteen 3⅜" squares. Cut each square in half diagonally to make thirty-two triangles. (for Pinwheel blocks)

From the plaid:
Two 3½" x 21" strips (for border)
Two 5½" x 20½" strips (for border)

From the backing fabric:
One 18" x 42" strip; recut into two 21" pieces
(for envelope back)

From the light-color lining fabric:
One 20½" x 26½" strip (for lining)

Instructions

Note: Use a 1/4" seam allowance throughout unless otherwise noted.

Create the Sham Top

1. Make eight 5½" x 5½" Plnwheel blocks referring to Building Blocks on page 31, except trim each triangle unit to measure 3" x 3".

2. Stitch the Pinwheel blocks into two rows of four blocks each. Press seams in one direction. Stitch the two rows together to complete the sham center. Press seam to one side.

3. Sew a 5¾" x 20½" plaid strip to the long sides of the sham center and the 3¾" x 21" plaid strips to the ends. Press seams toward the strips to complete the sham top.

4. Place the sham top right side up on the 20½" x 26½" lining strip. Pin all around.

5. Stitch around the outside edge, using a ⅛" seam allowance.

Finish the Sham

1. Turn one 21" edge of an 18" x 21" backing piece under ½" and press. Turn under the same edge another 1¼" and press. Stitch along the folded edge to sew the double-turn hem in place. Repeat with the remaining backing piece. (See Sewing Basics on page 95 for more information.)

2. Place the sham top right side up. Place the hemmed backing pieces right side down on the sham top, overlapping the hemmed edges to fit the top. Pin to hold.

3. Stitch around the outside edges using a ½" seam allowance.

4. Clip the corners and turn the sham right side out. Press.

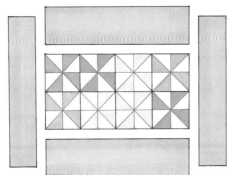

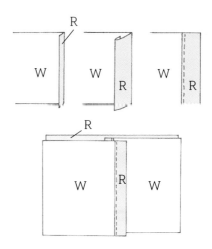

magic carpet

This **easy quilt** is perfect for any kind of **get-away activity—a nap** in a hammock, a picnic or maybe even to **hide under for a while!**

Finished Quilt Size: 52" x 58"
Finished Block Size: 6"
Skill Level: Beginner

Fabric

- Fat eighth or large scrap of 29 different fabrics (we chose gradated fabrics in five colors—turquoise, pink, red, yellow and green)
- 2¼ yards gray dot
- 1 yard navy solid
- 3¾ yards backing fabric

Supplies & Notions

- Twin-size batting (60" x 66" piece)
- Thread in colors to match fabrics
- Basting pins
- Basic sewing supplies

Cutting

From each of the 29 different fabrics:
One 6½" square (for A pieces in the Snowball blocks)

From the gray dot:
Eight 6½" x 42" strips; recut into forty-three 6½" squares
Eight 2½" x 42" strips; recut into one hundred sixteen 2½" squares
  (for B pieces in the Snowball blocks)

From the navy solid:
Six 2½" x 42" strips (for border)
Six 2½" x 42" strips (for binding)

Building Blocks

Make the Snowball Blocks

1. Draw a diagonal line on the back side of each B square.

2. Place a B square right sides together on each corner of an A square.

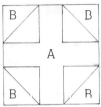

3. Stitch on the drawn lines. Trim seam allowances to ¼".

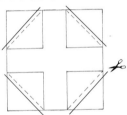

4. Press the B corners open to make one 6½" x 6½" block.

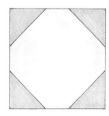

5. Repeat to make a total of 29 blocks.

Instructions

Note: Use a ¼″ seam allowance throughout.

Create the Quilt Top

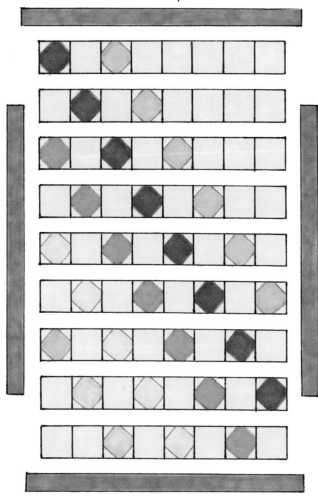

1. Using the Snowball blocks and the 6½″ gray dot squares, assemble nine rows of eight blocks and squares each. Press seams in alternating rows in opposite directions.

2. Stitch the rows together to assemble the quilt center. Press seams in one direction.

3. Stitch the 2½″ x 42″ navy solid border strips together on the short ends to make a long strip. Press seams to one side. Cut into two 54½″ strips and two 52½″ strips. Sew the longer strips to the long sides and the shorter strips to the top and bottom of the quilt center. Press seams toward the strips to complete the top.

Finish the Quilt

Note: Refer to Quilting in Sewing Basics on page 94 throughout the following steps.

1. Prepare a 60″ x 66″ backing piece.

2. Layer the backing fabric right side down, then the batting, and the quilt top right side up. Baste or pin layers together.

3. Quilt as desired.

4. Remove basting or pins. Trim on all sides.

5. Stitch the six 2½″ x 42″ binding strips short ends together to make one long strip.

6. Attach the binding to the edges of the quilt.

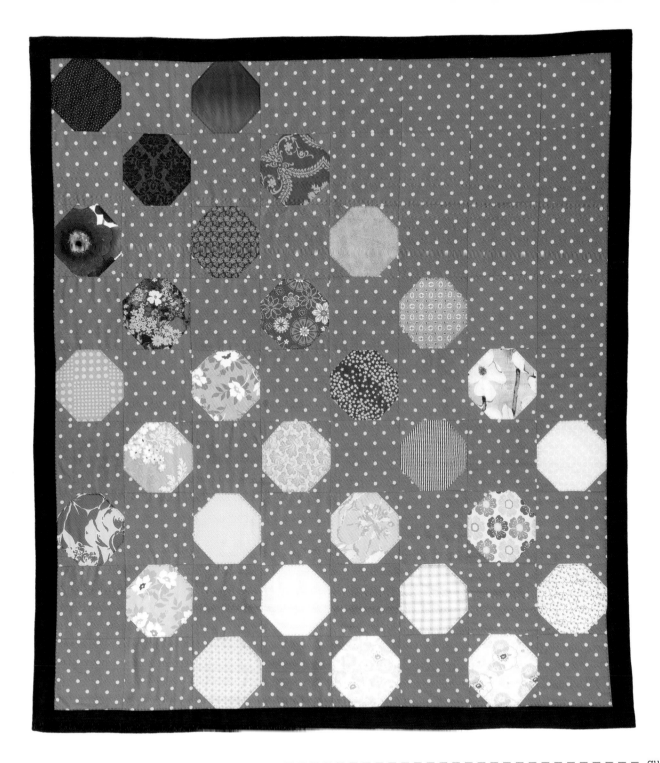

laptop case

Don't just **protect your laptop**—turn it into a **fashion statement** with this **great case.**

Finished Size: 11" x 15$\frac{1}{2}$"
Finished Block Size: 9"
Skill Level: Intermediate

Fabric

- 1 yard main fabric A
- $\frac{1}{2}$ yard lining fabric B
- $\frac{1}{4}$ yard Heart block fabric C
- $\frac{1}{3}$ yard duck canvas

Supplies & Notions

- $\frac{1}{2}$ yard high-loft batting
- Thread to match fabrics
- Three large buttons or 6" of 1"-wide hook and loop tape
- $\frac{1}{2}$ yard of 20"-wide iron-on interfacing
- Fabric marking pencil or pen
- Basic sewing supplies

Cutting for Either Case

Note: This case is for a 15" laptop. Increase or decrease sizes as needed if your laptop is larger or smaller.

From fabric A:
Note: Cut all pieces parallel to the selvage edge.
One 32" x 42" strip; recut into two 2" x 32" strips parallel to the selvage edge (for piece 1), two 3" x 15" pieces parallel to the selvage (for handles), one 10" x 5$\frac{1}{2}$" strip (for piece 2), one 10" x 18$\frac{1}{2}$" strip (for piece 3), and one 8" square (for closure tab)

From fabric B:
One 12" x 32" strip (for lining)

From the duck canvas:
Two 3" x 15" pieces (for handles)
One 8" square (for closure tab)

From the iron-on interfacing:

Two 3" x 15" pieces (for handles)
One 8" square (for closure tab)

From the high-loft batting:

One 12" x 32" piece

Additional Cutting for the Heart Case Only
From fabric A:

Two 5½" squares (for piece B in Heart block)
Four 2¾" squares (for piece A in Heart block)

From fabric C:

Two 5½" x 10" pieces (for piece C in Heart block)

Additional Cutting for the Nine-Patch Case Only
From fabric A:

Nine 4" squares cut diagonally on the fabric

Instructions

Use a ½" seam allowance throughout.

Preparation of Pieces

1. Following the manufacturer's instructions, adhere the iron-on interfacing to both 3" x 15" fabric A handle pieces and the 8" fabric A closure tab square.

2. Baste the duck canvas pieces to the wrong side of the fabric A handle pieces and closure tab square.

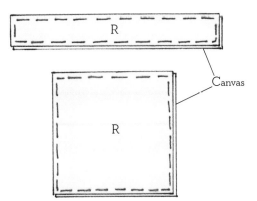

Make the Main Panel

1. Prepare a Heart block for the Heart Case or a Nine-Patch block for the Nine-Patch Case referring to Building Blocks on pages 69 and 71.

2. Stitch the 5½" x 10" piece 2 strip to the top of the quilt block and the 10" x 18½" piece 3 rectangle to the bottom of the quilt block. Press seams away from the block. Sew the 2" x 32" piece 1 strips to the long sides of the pieced unit. Press seams toward the strips.

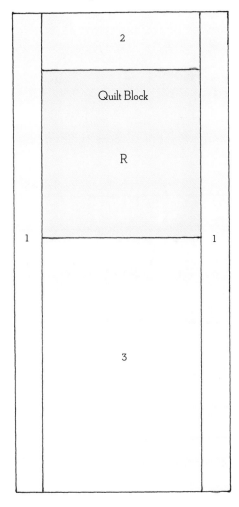

3. Place the pieced panel right side up on the batting. Baste in place close to the edge. Trim batting even with the edges of the panel.

Make the Handles

1. Fold the 3" x 15" fabric A handle pieces in half along the length and press. Fold both long edges to the creased centerline and press again. Stitch 1/8" from the long edges.

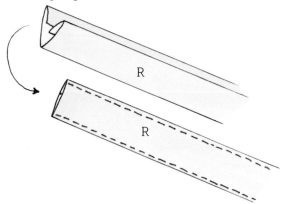

Make the Closure Tabs

1. For the Heart Case, fold the closure tab square in half with right sides together. Stitch the sides, leaving the bottom edge open for turning. Clip the corners and turn right side out. Press flat.

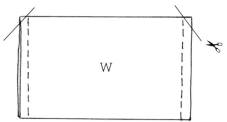

2. Find the center of the tab. Measure up 3/4" from the folded edge and make a mark with the marking pen or pencil. Make two more marks between this center mark and the sides. These will indicate the start points for your buttonholes.

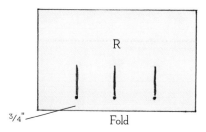

3. Make a buttonhole at each mark following the instructions in your sewing machine manual. For more information on buttonholes, see Closures in Sewing Basics on page 93.

4. For the Nine-Patch Case, fold the closure tab square in half with right sides together. Press to crease the center of the tab. Unfold the tab piece and lay flat. Center the 6" hook piece 1/2" from the fold line on the right side of the fabric. Stitch the hook piece in place, backtacking at the beginning and end of your stitching line.

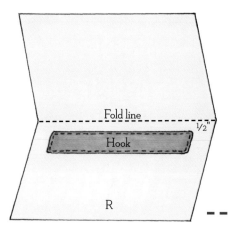

Building Blocks

- -

Make the Nine-Patch Blocks (for the Nine-Patch Case)

1. Stitch three 4" squares together to make a row. Press seams in one direction. Repeat to make a total of three rows.

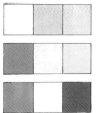

2. Stitch the rows together to complete one 10" x 10" block. Press seams in one direction.

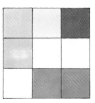

5. Repeat step 1 to complete the tab.

Finish the Case

1. Pin the tab closure piece in the center of the bottom end of the main panel, aligning raw edges. Pin the raw ends of the handles at the seams between pieces 1 and 3 at each end of the panel. Baste the handles and tab closure piece in place.

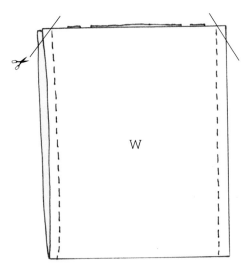

2. Fold main panel in half across the width with right sides together. Stitch along the sides of the panel, backtacking at the end of each stitching line. Clip corners.

3. Fold the fabric B lining strip in half across the width with right sides together. Stitch along the sides, leaving a 5″ opening on one side for turning. Clip corners and turn right side out.

4. Tuck the lining into the main panel with right sides together and the handles and closure tab between the layers. Line up the side seams and top edge and pin in place. Stitch around the top edge.

5. Turn the case right side out through the opening in the lining, slipstitch the opening closed and tuck the lining into the case. See Slipstitch instructions on page 92.

6. For the Heart Case, slip the laptop into the case. Bring the closure tab to the front of the case and make a mark through each buttonhole for button positions. Stitch a button at each mark to finish the case. See Sewing Buttons instructions on page 93.

7. For the Nine-Patch Case, slip the laptop into the case. Bring the closure tab to the front of the case. Fold the tab back to the edge of the hook piece. Mark along the edge of the hook piece for the loop piece position. Securely whipstitch the loop piece in place on the case front to finish the case. See Whipstitch instructions on page 92.

Building Blocks

- -

Make the Heart Block (for the Heart Case)

1. Draw a diagonal line on the back side of all A and B squares.

2. Place an A square right sides together on two corners of each C piece and a B square on the bottom.

3. Stitch on the drawn lines. Trim seam allowances to ¼".

4. Press the A and B corners open.

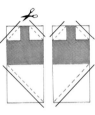

5. Sew the two halves together, matching the A square seams, to make one 10" x 10" Heart block.

gift ideas

note card holder

A note card holder is a **wonderful shower gift**—a place to keep cards for a new baby's arrival or a wedding as a **memento of the special event.**

Finished Size: 8″ x 10″ closed,
24″ x 10″ open
Finished Block Size: 6″
Skill Level: Intermediate

Fabric for Tan Nine-Patch Holder

- 2/3 yard tan ticking print
- 1/2 yard brown print
- 5/8 yard light blue dot
- 1/8 yard cream print
- 1/2 yard duck canvas

Fabric for Red Dot String Bean Holder

- 2/3 yard red dot
- 5/8 yard fuchsia floral
- Fat eighth light green print
- 1/4 yard turquoise solid
- 1/2 yard duck canvas

Supplies & Notions

- Thread to match fabrics
- Felt or batting

- One 1″ button (for tan holder tab closure)
- 1/4 yard 22″-wide iron-on interfacing (for tan holder tab closure)
- Basic sewing supplies

Cutting for Tan Holder

From the tan ticking print:
Three 2½″ x 42″ strips; recut into two 2½″ x 6½″ pieces (for piece 2), two 2½″ x 24½″ strips (for piece 3), and one 2½″ x 20″ strip (for closure tab)
One 10½″ x 42″ strip; recut into one 10½″ x 24½″ piece (for lining) and two 1½″ x 6½″ pieces (for piece 1)

From the brown print:
One 10½″ x 24½″ piece (for lining) and nine 2½″ squares (for Nine-Patch blocks)

From the light blue dot:
One 2½″ x 20½″ strip (for closure tab)
One 12″ x 24½″ piece (for inside pocket)
Nine 2½″ squares (for quilt blocks)

From the cream print:
One 2½″ x 42″ strip; recut into nine 2½″ squares (for Nine-Patch blocks)

From the iron-on interfacing:
One 2½″ x 20″ strip

Cutting for Red Dot Holder

From the red dot:
Two 1½″ x 42″ strips; recut into one 1½″ x 29″ strip (for tie), one 1½″ x 15″ strip (for tie), and two 1½″ x 6½″ pieces (for piece 1)
Two 2½″ x 42″ strips; recut into two 2½″ x 6½″ pieces (for piece 2) and two 2½″ x 24½″ strips (for piece 3)
One 10½″ x 24½″ piece (for lining)

From the fuchsia floral:

One 12" x 42" strip; recut into one 12" x 24½" piece (for inside pocket) and two 6⅞ squares. Cut the squares in half diagonally to make A triangles (for String Bean blocks).

Two 1½" x 42" strips; recut into one 1½" x 29" strip (for tie lining) and one 1½" x 15" strip (for tie lining)

From the light green print:

One 6⅞" x 21" strip; recut into two 6⅞" squares. Cut the squares in half diagonally to make B triangles (for String Bean blocks).

From the turquoise solid:

One 3½" x 42" strip; recut into six 3½" C squares (for String Bean blocks)

Cutting for Either Option

From the duck canvas:

One 10½" x 24½" piece for each holder

From the batting or felt:

One 12" x 27" piece for each holder

Instructions

Use a ¼" seam allowance throughout

Create the Outside Panel

1. Stitch the three quilt blocks together with pieces 1 and 2. Press seams away from the quilt blocks. Sew a piece 3 to the long sides of the pieced strip to complete the panel. Press seams toward the piece 3 strips.

3					
1	Quilt Bock	2	Quilt Bock	2	Quilt Bock	1
3					

2. Sandwich the batting or felt between the wrong side of the panel and the duck canvas piece. Baste around the perimeter as close to the edge as possible.

3. Stitch in the ditch around each quilt block.

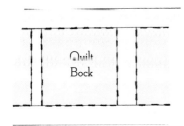

Make Closure

1. For the red dot holder tie closure, place the 1¹/₂" x 29" red dot and fuchsia floral strips right sides together and stitch both long edges and one short edge. Clip the corners, turn right side out and press. Repeat with the 1¹/₂" x 15" tie pieces.

2. Baste ties in place at the center of one end of the outside panel.

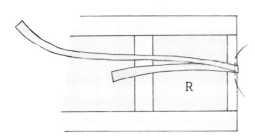

3. For the tan holder tab closure, follow the manufacturer's instructions and adhere the iron-on interfacing to the wrong side of the tan ticking closure tab.

4. Place the 2¹/₂" x 20" tan ticking and light blue dot tab pieces right sides together and stitch both long edges and one short edge. Clip the corners, turn right side out and press.

5. Baste tab in place at the center of one end of the outside panel with the blue dot side against the block side of the panel.

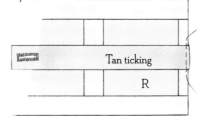

Inside Pocket and Lining

1. Fold the inside pocket piece along the length with right sides together.

Building Blocks

- - - - - - - - - - - - - - - -

Make the Nine-Patch Blocks
(for the tan holder)

1. Stitch a blue dot, brown print and cream print 2¹/₂" square together to make a row. Press seams in one direction. Repeat to make a total of three rows, varying placement of fabrics from row to row.

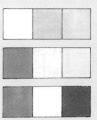

2. Stitch the rows together to complete one 6¹/₂" x 6¹/₂" block.

3. Repeat to make a total of three blocks.

2. Draw stitching lines along the length of the strip. Stitch along the drawn lines.

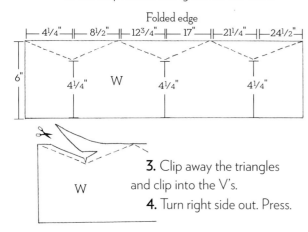

Folded edge

4¼" — 8½" — 12¾" — 17" — 21¼" — 24½"

6"

4¼"   W   4¼"   4¼"

3. Clip away the triangles and clip into the V's.

4. Turn right side out. Press.

W

5. Place the pocket piece on top of the right side of the lining piece matching the side and bottom edges. Baste in place as close to the outer edge as possible.

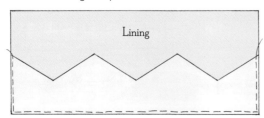

Lining

Finish the Holder

1. With right sides together, stitch the lining/pocket piece to the outside panel around the outside edges, sandwiching the ties or tab closure between the layers. Leave a 4″ opening on the end opposite the ties or tab closure.

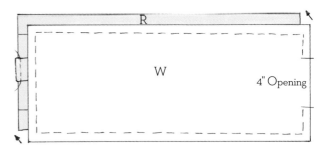

R

W

4" Opening

2. Clip corners. Turn right side out through the opening. Turn the opening edges to the inside. Press. Slipstitch the opening closed. See Sewing Basics, page 92.

3. Stitch all layers together vertically at each peak of the inside pocket to create individual pockets. Backtack at the beginning and end of each stitching line.

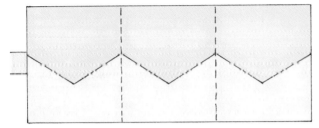

Add the Button

1. For the tan holder, sew the button on the tab closure about 1¼" from the inner edge on the tan ticking side. Refer to Sewing Buttons instructions on page 93.

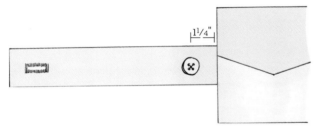

2. Close the note card holder and mark the placement for the buttonhole. Make sure that it's not too tight so there's room for cards and envelopes!

3. Make a buttonhole. Clip the fabric in the center of the buttonhole with a seam ripper or small scissors. (See Sewing Basics, page 93.)

Building Blocks

Make the String Bean Blocks (for the red dot holder)

1. Stitch an A triangle to a B triangle on the long side. Open and press seam toward the A triangle.

2. Draw a diagonal line on the back side of each C square.

3. Place a C square right sides together on the A corner of the pieced unit. Stitch on the drawn line. Trim seam allowance to ¼".

4. Press the C corner open.

5. Repeat on the B corner to complete one 6½" x 6½" block.

6. Repeat to make a total of three blocks.

tiny charm bags

These charms make **playful little gifts.** Just add a **special note** or a **tiny surprise inside.** Or use them to **spice up** any **key chain** or tote!

Finished Size: Approximately 3" x 5"
Skill Level: Intermediate

Fabric

- One or more scraps for each charm bag

Supplies & Notions

- Thread in colors to match fabrics
- Hand sewing needle
- Iron-on interfacing
- 3/8"–1/2" button
- Small embellishments (optional)
- Basic sewing supplies

Cutting

From the fabric scraps:

One 1½" x 5" piece per bag (for hanging loop)
Bag pieces as directed in instructions

Instructions

Use a 1/4" seam allowance throughout.

Prepare the Bag Pieces

1. Make templates for the pieces of the chosen bag shape using the patterns given on the pull-out pattern sheets.

2. Trace two back pieces and two pocket flap pieces on the wrong side of the chosen fabric scraps. Cut out each piece, adding a 1/4" seam allowance all around each shape.

3. Fold another fabric scrap in half with right sides together. Place the pocket template on the scrap with the straight edge of the template on the fabric fold. Trace and cut out through both layers, adding a 1/4" seam allowance to the sides of the pocket.

4. Cut out one back piece and one pocket flap piece from iron-on interfacing. Adhere the interfacing pieces to the wrong side of one fabric back piece and one fabric pocket flap piece.

5. Trace and cut out two leaf pieces, if desired. Place the pieces right sides together. Stitch around the outside edges, leaving a 1" opening for turning. Turn the leaf right side out. Fold the opening edges to the inside. Press. Slip-stitch the opening closed.

6. Fold the hanging loop strip under 1/2" on both long edges. Press. Fold in half along the length. Press and stitch 1/8" from the edge on both long sides.

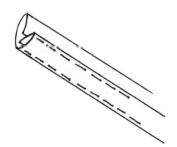

Creating the Pocket Panel

1. Place the two pocket flap pieces right sides together and stitch along the curved bottom edge. Clip close to the seam, turn right side out and press the sewn edge to make a smooth curve.

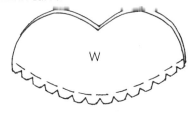

2. Make a buttonhole in the pocket flap piece to fit your button, starting as close to the bottom edge of the flap piece as possible.

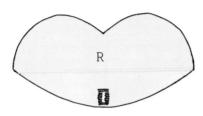

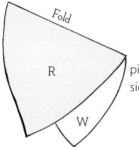

3. Fold the pocket piece in half with right side out. Press.

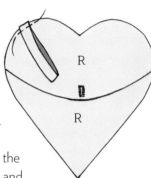

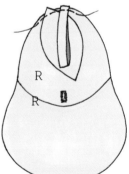

4. Place the pocket piece on the right side of the back piece without the interfacing, matching the bottom edges. Place the pocket flap on top of the pocket/back unit, matching the top edge. Pin together. Stitch in place ⅛" from outer edges.

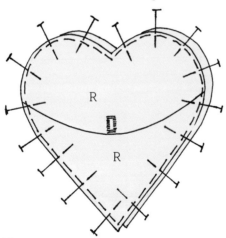

Finishing the Charm

1. Fold the hanging loop strip in half. Pin to the right side of the pocket panel with raw edges even. Baste in place.

2. Place the leaf next to the hanging loop, if applicable, and baste in place.

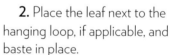

3. Place the pocket panel right sides together with the interfaced back piece, sandwiching the hanging loop and leaf between the layers. Stitch around the outside edge, leaving a 1″ opening for turning.

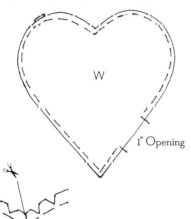

1″ Opening

4. Clip around the edge close to the stitching line and into the V at the top of the heart.

5. Turn right sides out and press. As you press, pinch the seam and roll it between your fingers to get a crisp, curved edge. Turn the opening edges to the inside and slipstitch the opening closed.

6. Make a mark in the center of the buttonhole. Use this mark to position your button and sew on the button. (See Sewing Buttons, page 93.)

7. To add embellishments to the back of the charm, pin the decoration into place and whipstitch around the edges, being careful to catch only one layer of fabric in your stitches!

fabric flowers

These **adorable little flowers** are a great way to **use up scraps. Add extra adornment** to purses, sweaters, or anything that could use a **spot of extra color!**

Finished Size: Approximately 6″
Skill Level: Beginner

Fabric

- Scrap fabric A
- Fat eighth fabric B
- Fat eighth fabric C

Supplies & Notions

- Thread to match fabrics
- Decorative button
- Pin back or hair clip (optional)
- Basic sewing supplies

Cutting

Note: Prepare templates for the flower Back, Center and Petal shapes using patterns given on the pull-out pattern sheets. Mark shapes on the wrong sides of the fabrics and cut out, adding a ¼″ seam allowance around each piece when cutting.

From fabric A:
Two center pieces

From fabric B:
Fourteen petal pieces

From fabric C:
Two back pieces

Instructions

Use a 1/4" seam allowance throughout.

Construct the petals

1. Place the center pieces right sides together. Stitch around on the marked line, leaving a 1" opening for turning. Clip the seam allowance. Turn right side out. Turn the opening edges in and press. Slipstitch the opening closed. (See Sewing Basics, page 92.)

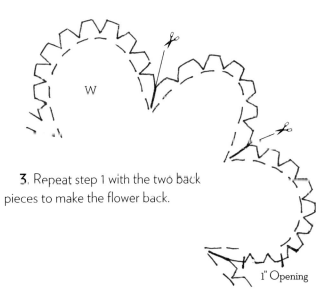

3. Repeat step 1 with the two back pieces to make the flower back.

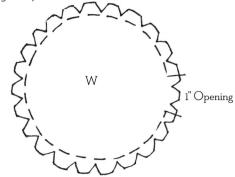

2. Repeat step 1 with two petal pieces, leaving the straight end open, to make one petal. Repeat to make seven petals.

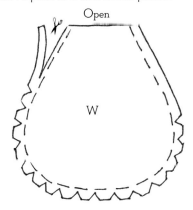

Add Gathering

1. Sew a long gathering stitch around the center of the center circle, leaving long thread tails. Do not backtack. The stitched circle should be about the size of a quarter.

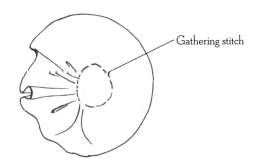

Gathering stitch

2. Pull the top thread to gather the circle. Knot the thread ends so the gathers don't loosen.

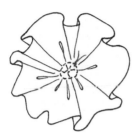

3. Stitch the petals into an overlapping chain, using a gathering stitch and back-tacking at the start only. Leave long thread tails. Repeat to make a second line of stitches 1/8" from the first stitching line. Pull the two top threads to gather the petals.

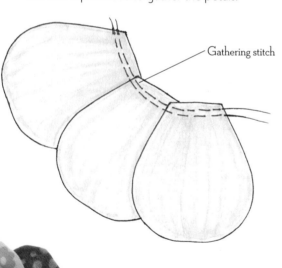

Gathering stitch

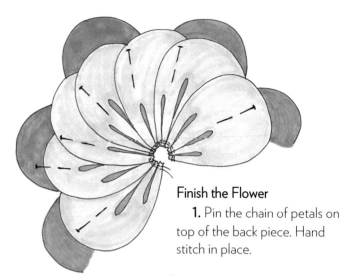

Finish the Flower

1. Pin the chain of petals on top of the back piece. Hand stitch in place.

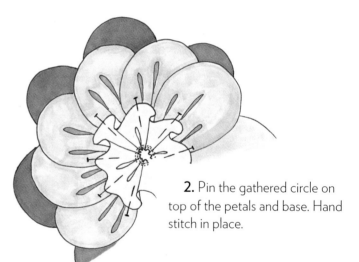

2. Pin the gathered circle on top of the petals and base. Hand stitch in place.

3. Add the decorative button on top of all the layers.

4. Optional: Stitch a pin back or hair clip to the back of the flower to make a decorative pin for your jacket or bag or a decoration for your hair.

scrappy jars

Do you have a bunch of jars that are on their way to be recycled?
Take recycling a step further—put them to use as **lively accents**
for decorating or to give as gifts. **No sewing required!**

You'll need:

- Clean, dry jars with labels removed
- Fabric scraps
- White craft glue
- Clear protective finish
- Flat 1"–2" paintbrush

Instructions

1. Cut a piece of fabric to fit around the jar, adding $1/2$" for overlap.
2. Paint glue onto the wrong side of the fabric piece.
3. Place the strip around the jar, working out bubbles with your fingers.
4. Let dry.
5. Paint clear finish over the fabric; do not get it on the glass.
6. Let dry. It's finished!

scrappy note cards

Need a **quick card for any holiday?** How about **unique thank-you notes** or invitations? Scrappy Note Cards could be **the answer!**

Finished Size: Varies
Skill Level: Beginner

Fabric

- Print scraps

Supplies & Notions

- One 5¹⁄₂″ x 7¹⁄₂″ piece of card stock per card (or size of choice)
- Envelope to fit card
- Thread to match fabric scraps
- Scrap of iron-on interfacing
- Scrap of fusible web
- Glue stick
- Basic sewing supplies

Instructions

Making the Card Base

1. Subtract 1/2" from the height and width of your card. Since we used cards that are 5 1/2" x 7 1/2" our measurement is 5" x 7". Cut a piece this size from a fabric scrap and the iron-on interfacing.

2. Following the manufacturer's instructions, adhere the iron-on interfacing to the wrong side of the fabric rectangle.

Adding the Decoration

1. Using the patterns given for the Tiny Charm Bags on the pull-out pattern sheets or a pattern of

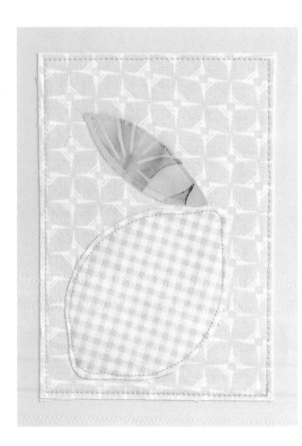

choice, trace or photocopy the design you'd like to use. If you're making small cards, you may need to reduce the size of the shape.

2. Trace the patterns on the paper side of the fusible web scrap, leaving 1/8"–1/4" between the shapes. Cut out the shapes, leaving a margin all around. Fuse to the wrong side of the chosen fabric scraps.

3. Cut out the shapes on the drawn lines. Remove the paper backings.

4. Position the appliqué pieces on the interfaced fabric rectangle. Fuse in place. Stitch 1/8" from the edge all around. **Note:** Change the top thread to match your appliqué pieces as necessary.

Finish the Note Card

1. Make a few lines with the glue stick on the card stock piece. Center the appliquéd fabric rectangle on top with 1/4" of the card stock showing on all sides.

2. Put the card on a flat surface, under a heavy book for a few minutes.

3. Stitch around the fabric rectangle 1/8" from the edge.

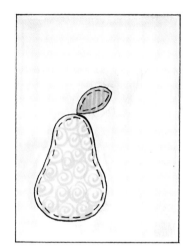

1/4"

gift ideas

scarf

A French seam gives this **light spring scarf** a touch of **elegance.** Choose from the wide range of trims available to **customize to your look or style.**

Finished Size: *26" x 67" triangle*
Skill Level: *Intermediate*

Fabric

- 1¼ yards blue and white embroidered print
- ¾ yard blue and white floral
- ¾ yard white dotted Swiss

Supplies & Notions

- Thread to match fabrics
- 2½ yards trim (We used small white ball trim)
- Craft paper for pattern drafting
- Straight pins
- Basic sewing supplies

Instructions

Use a ¼" seam allowance throughout unless otherwise noted.

Prepare the Patterns and Cut the Pieces

1. Draw a 68" horizontal line with a 27" vertical centerline. It should look like a T. Connect the end points of the T.

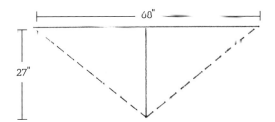

2. Make parallel lines 8" and 18" from one diagonal edge. Add marks so you can match up the edges of the fabric when pinning them together

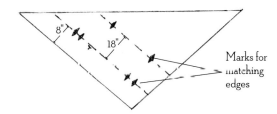

Marks for matching edges

3. Cut the pattern apart to make pieces.

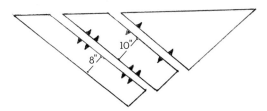

4. On the blue and white embroidered print, trace around the 8"-wide pattern piece, marking the notches. Cut out piece 1 along the drawn lines.

5. On the blue and white floral, trace around the 10"-wide pattern piece, marking the notches. Cut out piece 2 along the drawn lines.

6. On the white dotted Swiss, trace around the triangle pattern piece, marking the notches. Cut out piece 3 along the drawn lines.

Sidebar

French seams are often used for light-weight fabrics. It is a seam that is sewn twice. To create a French seam, follow these instructions:

1. Place the two fabrics WRONG sides together and sew using a 1/4" seam allowance.

2. Trim the seam allowance and press the seam to one side.

3. Fold the fabric with right sides together to sandwich the raw seam edges between the right sides of the fabric.

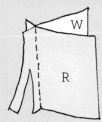 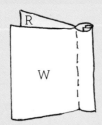

4. Press the fold to create a sharp, clean edge.

5. Stitch a second seam parallel to your first sewing line, about 1/4" from the edge of the fabric. Press to one side. This leaves a seam that looks clean and finished from both sides.

Assemble the Scarf

1. Stitch the scarf pieces together using French seams and matching the marked notches. Remember to backtack at the end of each stitching line.

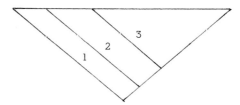

Hem the Edges

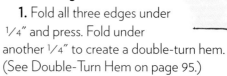

1. Fold all three edges under 1/4" and press. Fold under another 1/4" to create a double-turn hem. (See Double-Turn Hem on page 95.)

2. Press and pin to hold.

3. Topstitch around the outside edges of the triangle, removing the pins as you go. Press.

Add Trim

1. Pin trim to the wrong side of the scarf.

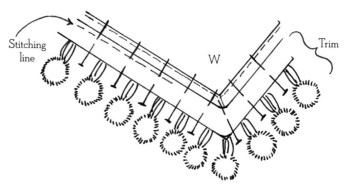

2. Stitch in place, making sure to backtack at the start and finish.

Backtack – A way of securing a machine-sewn seam. To create a backtack, start sewing a seam, stitching only 3 or 4 stitches, and stop. Press the "reverse" lever on your sewing machine, and stitch backwards over the stitches you just created. Let go of the reverse lever, and stitch forward for the rest of the seam. To backtack at the end of a seam, repeat this process in reverse.

Baste – To attach two fabrics together temporarily using an extra-long stitch. The length of the stitch makes it easier to remove later.

Batting – The center layer of a quilt. It creates the thickness of the quilt. The higher the loft, the thicker and fluffier your quilt. It is available in cotton, polyester, silk, wool, bamboo and blends.

Bias – A fabric edge cut at a 45° angle to the grain of the fabric. Fabric runs from selvage to sselvage with fibers running at 90 degrees to one another. A bias edge is cut diagonally across this grain. This often happens when cutting triangles. The bias edge is prone to stretching and should be handled carefully.

Facing – A piece of fabric sewn onto the back of another, more visible, piece of fabric. The facing allows for the raw edge of the front fabric to be finished with the raw edge hidden between the two pieces of fabric.

Fat eighth – A precut fabric rectangle that measures 9" x 21". These pieces are usually available in a variety of colors and prints at fabric and quilt shops.

Fat quarter – A precut fabric rectangle that measures 18" x 21". These pieces are usually available in a variety of colors and prints at fabric and quilt shops

Fiberfill – Soft filling for stuffing dimensional projects, such as blocks and pillows.

Fusible Web – A product that consists of a sheet of adhesive webbing on a paper liner or between two paper liners. It is most often used for machine appliqué to attach the appliqué shape to the background fabric.

Grain – The lengthwise grain runs the length of woven fabrics, parallel to the selvage edge. The crosswise grain runs across woven fabrics, from selvage edge to selvage edge. It is important to cut pieces for handbag handles and apparel pieces along the lengthwise grain, unless otherwise noted.

Iron-on Interfacing – A sew-in or fusible product that gives support to lightweight fabrics and pieces that need extra stability; i.e., handles, buttonhole tabs, etc.

R – These abbreviations marked on the diagrams indicate the right side of the fabric or project.

Seam Allowance – The distance between the raw edge of the fabric and the line of stitching. When quilting, a $1/4$" seam allowance is generally used. Other types of sewing require a $1/2$" or $5/8$" seam allowance. It is very important to pay attention to instructions when seam allowances are referenced, as it is crucial to use the proper seam allowance to get patterns to come out properly. In this book, we use $1/4$" and $1/2$" seam allowances. Each project will state what width to use.

Selvage – The narrow, woven edge that runs along the outermost edges of a fabric. There is often information on these edges. It may include the name of the fabric collection and the fabric designer's name, and there are often colored dots on the edge as well. These dots indicate every dye color that was used in printing the fabric and are helpful when finding matching fabrics for a project. The selvage edge should never be used in your project.

Staystitch – A second line of stitching applied parallel to a first line, usually during the sewing process. The second line allows the sewing to remain stable and to preserve the shape as more features are being sewn in.

Stitch in the Ditch – Stitching in the seam between two fabrics, usually to help hide the stitching lines. This is most often done to quilt multiple layers of fabric and batting together.

Topstitch – Stitching that shows on the top or outside of a project. This is often used to keep layers in place, or to make layered fabrics to lie more evenly on a finished project. It is best to increase the stitch length slightly when topstitching.

W – These abbreviations marked on the diagrams indicate the wrong side of the fabric or project.

glossary

Hand Embroidery Stitches

Backstitch

The backstitch is well named; the idea of this stitch is that you work backward to create the stitch that will show on the front of your fabric.

1. Make a knot in your thread, and bring your needle to the front side of the fabric from the back.
2. Make a small stitch forward and push your needle to the back of the fabric.
3. Bring the needle through to the front side of the fabric, about a stitch length ahead in the line of stitching.
4. Push the needle back through the fabric at the end of the first stitch, so the thread stitches backward to fill in the stitch space.
5. For the next stitch, bring the needle through to the front of the fabric a bit ahead in the stitch line from the one just made, and stitch backward to fill the gap.
6. Repeat along the entire line of stitching.

Backstitch

Blanket Stitch

The blanket stitch is great for adding appliqué because the stitch can rest on the edge of the appliqué piece and function to hold the piece in place while adding decoration to the appliqué.

1. Make a knot in your thread, and bring it from the back of your fabric to the front. If using it for appliqué, it should come through about 1/8" in from the edge of the appliqué piece.
2. Make the first stitch by pushing the needle through the fabric about 1/8" to the right of its current position.
3. Pull most of the thread through, but leave a small loop in the stitch.
4. Put your needle through this small loop, from the back to the front.

5. Pull the stitch tight.
6. Make the next stitch to the right of the one just completed and repeat the same motion.
7. At the end of the appliqué, join the last stitch to the first by bringing the thread through the first blanket stitch, then tie it off at the back of the fabric.

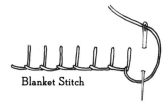

Blanket Stitch

Slipstitch

The slipstitch is used to stitch a folded edge to a flat piece of fabric and is often used for hems.

1. Cut a length of thread suitable for your seam. Thread a needle and place a knot in the end of the thread.
2. Bring the thread through to the front, from underneath the folded edge of fabric, so that the knot is hidden underneath the fold.
3. Place the bulk of the stitch on the folded edge of the fabric and create nearly straight stitches, allowing the thread to dip into the straight piece of fabric just enough to catch a thread or two of the fabric.

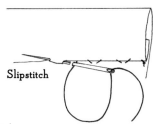

Slipstitch

Whipstitch

A whipstitch is often used to close a hem.

1. Pin the fabric or hem in place.
2. Cut a length of thread suitable for your seam length. Thread the needle and make a knot in the end of the thread.
3. Bring the thread through the fabric at the start of the seam, so that the knot rests just inside the seam and hidden from view.

4. Place your needle through the top layer of the fabric just at the fold where it meets the bottom layer. Make your stitch at an angle to the fold and angle the needle so that it comes out of the bottom layer just at the fold.

5. Repeat this process along the seam.

Whipstitch

Appliqué

Faced Appliqué

A faced appliqué is an appliqué piece that has fabric attached as a backing to finish raw edges. Lightweight white solid, muslin, the same fabric as the appliqué piece, or a fabric that contrasts with the appliqué piece are all good choices for the backing fabric (facing fabric).

1. Prepare a template for each appliqué shape using the pattern given.

2. Place the template on the wrong side of the chosen fabric. Trace around the shape.

3. Cut out the appliqué shape, adding a 1/4" seam allowance all around.

4. Place the fabric shape right sides together with the facing fabric. Cut out the facing piece. Leave the pieces right sides together with the appliqué piece on top.

5. Stitch on the marked line on the appliqué piece.

6. Clip the corners and any curves as applicable. Cut a slit in the facing piece. Be careful to cut the facing fabric only.

Faced Appliqué

7. Turn the shape right side out through the slit and poke out the corners. Press.

8. Attach the appliqué piece to your project using a straight stitch close to the shape edges or use a decorative machine stitch.

Machine Appliqué

A machine blanket stitch or satin stitch is a quick and easy way to attach a raw-edged appliqué piece to a project while still making sure that the edge will be covered. Most fabrics will require a stabilizer for this technique. In general, an iron-on or tear-away stabilizer will work best.

1. Pin or fuse the stabilizer to the back of the base fabric.

2. Select the stitch. Starting on a side, stitch the appliqué shape down. If your machine offers it, using the needle-down feature is wonderful for turning corners on appliqué shapes. Consult your machine manual for details.

3. At the end of your stitching, use a locking stitch if your machine offers it. If not, sew your last stitch on top of your first stitch.

4. If the thread or stitching is very visible and you don't want to overlap a stitch, use a hand-sewing needle to tie off the ends. Leave an extra long tail of thread when removing from the machine. Thread the top thread through the needle and stitch it through to the back. Tie off the needle and bobbin thread with a traditional sewing knot on the back of the project.

Machine Blanket Stitch

Closures

Sewing Buttons

1. Mark the location for your button.

2. Cut a length of thread about 24" long. Thread it through a hand-sewing needle. Double the thread on itself, and tie a knot in the end.

3. Thread the needle through the right side of the fabric at the button location.

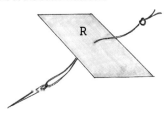

4. Place your button at the proper location and place a toothpick behind the button to hold it slightly away from the fabric.

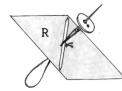

5. Pass the thread through to the front side of the fabric up through the hole of the button, down through the next hole in the button, and then back through the fabric.

6. Bring the thread to the front of the fabric and pass through another hole of the button (this will vary depending on how many holes your button has or whether you are using a shank button).

7. Repeat steps 5 and 6 several times.

8. Bring your thread forward from the back of the fabric, but keep it under the button.

9. Wrap the thread around the stitching a few times, then pass it through to the back of the fabric. Remove the toothpick.

10. Pass the needle through a few of the stitches and form a loop, then pass the needle through the loop to form a knot. Trim the thread close to the knot.

Making a Buttonhole

Most sewing machines offer a buttonhole feature. Check your machine manual for specific instructions. A few tips will help make sewing buttonholes easier.

• Use a buttonhole foot. This foot generally comes with the machine, and will allow the fabric to flow evenly under the needle.
• Mark all buttonholes the length that you want. This will help you to visualize the buttonhole before it is sewn. Trust us, buttonholes are not fun to rip out and re-do!
• Make practice buttonholes on a swatch of the fabric that you are using. This will help you get used to the order in which your machine stitches the buttonhole (does it go forward first, or backward), allow you to troubleshoot the size of the buttonhole, and let you make adjustments before the buttonhole is finished.
• Be sure to place pins at the ends of the buttonhole opening when cutting the fabric in the center. This will prevent accidents, like cutting the buttonhole past the stitched edges.

Installing a Magnetic Closure
1. Identify where the closure will be located. You may need to consult the pattern, or align the fabric pieces indicated to mark the spot for the closure. Some instructions or fabrics will call for the closure location to be lined with canvas or interfacing. Follow the specific instructions for the project.
2. Set one of the washers (this is one of the metal pieces that the prongs will go through) on the location, and mark the lines for the prongs. It is easiest to use a pencil or marker and to draw inside the actual holes of the washer to indicate the size of the holes you will need to make.

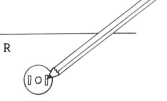

3. Use a piece of felt or canvas to stabilize the fabric behind the magnetic closure. Make a mark in the center of the canvas or felt as well.
4. Cut holes in the fabric and the canvas or felt for threading the metal prongs. Be careful not to cut the hole too large.

5. Place the washer on the back of the fabric and thread the pronged magnet side of the closure through the fabric, the canvas or felt, and the washer.

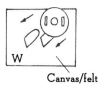

Canvas/felt

6. Use a pair of pliers or other strong hard tool to bend the prongs, securing the closure in place.

Canvas/felt

7. Repeat the steps above to insert the other side of the magnetic closure.

Quilting
Creating the Quilt Backing
The quilts in this book can all be made with two lengths of 42"-wide fabric.

1. Trim the selvage edges from the fabric required for the backing
2. Cut the fabric length in half. Sew the two fabric lengths together using a 1/2" seam allowance.

Basting the Quilt
1. Place your quilt backing right side down on a large flat surface.
2. Place the batting evenly on top of the backing.
3. Center the quilt top right side up on these two layers, taking care to eliminate any wrinkles.
4. Beginning in the center, place basting pins (large safety pins) 3"–4" apart across the entire quilt surface. Or make large basting stitches across the entire quilt surface.
5. Quilt as desired, then trim the batting and backing even with the quilt top.

Binding
The quilts made in this book are made with double-fold, straight-grain binding (this binding is made with strips cut across the width of the fabric).

1. Cut the number of binding strips in the width indicated in the pattern.
2. Stitch the strips short ends together to make one long binding strip with diagonal seams. To do this, place your binding strips with right sides together, perpendicular to each other. Mark a line on the top strip, from the upper left corner to the lower right edge of the strip. Sew on the drawn line. Trim the seam allowance to 1/4" and press the seam allowance open.

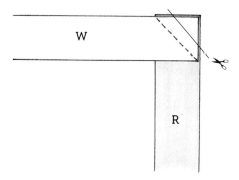

3. Press the binding strip in half along the length with wrong sides together.

Attaching the Binding
A walking foot is a wonderful sewing accessory to have for attaching binding to a quilt. It ensures that the fabric layers are fed evenly to avoid distortion of the quilt top.

1. Start the binding several inches from a corner of the quilt top. Leave at least 6" as a tail and align the raw edge of the folded binding strip with the edge of the quilt top.
2. Stitch the binding in place with a 1/4" seam allowance.
3. When you come to a corner, stop and backstitch 1/4" from the corner of the quilt top.

4. Remove the quilt from the machine. Fold the binding up to form a 45° angle away from the quilt top.

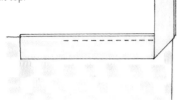

5. Hold this corner fold with one hand, and fold the binding strip back down and onto the quilt top, aligning the unstitched edge with the next side of the quilt top.

6. Stitch the binding beginning at the fold, and backstitch to secure the seam.

7. Continue stitching the binding to the quilt top as indicated above around the entire outer edge until you are about 6″ from the starting point of the binding.

8. Fold under one edge of the binding strip 1″ and finger press to create a clean edge.

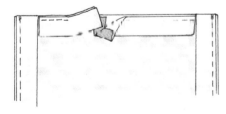

9. Insert the raw end of the binding into the folded end. Finish sewing to the starting point.

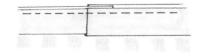

10. Turn the folded edge of the binding strip to the back of the quilt and slipstitch in place with a hand-sewing needle. When you reach corners, stitch the mitered binding edges closed.

General Sewing Techniques
Clipping Corners
We clip the corners of two sewn pieces when they are sewn right sides together and need to be turned right side out. This reduces bulk so that the corners can be poked out to a crisp point.

1. To clip corners, fold the corner so that the two perpendicular sides are aligned.

2. Clip off the end of the point, being careful not to get too close to the stitching line.

Gathering
1. Set the stitch length on your machine to the longest possible stitch. This is called a basting stitch.

2. Leave a thread tail about 4″ long. Start sewing at the edge of the fabric, and sew a straight line 1/8″ in from the edge, without backtacking. Leave a 4″ thread tail at the end of the seam.

3. Stitch another line 1/4″ from the edge, leaving 4″ thread tails at the beginning and end of the stitching line.

4. Find the top threads. Very gently pull on these tails so that the fabric begins cinching up in the center. Gather the fabric along the entire edge in this manner, until the width has been reduced to the desired measurement.

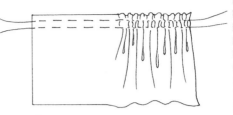

5. Even the gathers along the length. Knot the top and bottom threads together to secure the ends of the threads.

Double-Turn Hem
The double-turn hem is used so that there are no raw edges exposed.

1. To create a double-turn hem, start by folding the desired edge under 1/4″. Press.

2. Fold the fabric under again 1″, so that the first folded edge is enclosed in the new fold. Press. Stitch this hem down by placing your stitches 1/8″–1/4″ from the second (inner) fold line. This will ensure that both hems are enclosed in the seam.

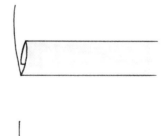

About the Authors

Kaitlin and Alison met in college when chance made them freshman year roommates. There they spent many enjoyable hours crafting, decorating their dorm room, and combing the racks at Goodwill for clothes to reconstruct.

Kaitlin showed an early interest in sewing and design after her grandmother and mother taught her the basics of the craft. She continued to follow her interest into college and graduated with a degree in Fine Art and Costume Design. After graduating, she worked for several theaters before moving to the west coast where she worked for Pacific Fabrics and Crafts in Seattle, Washington. It was here that she completely fell in love with textiles and hasn't looked back since! Kaitlin currently lives in Brooklyn, New York, with five sewing machines and tons of fabric.

Alison learned to sew at an early age but didn't take up the hobby in earnest until she was in her twenties. Her passion for sewing lies in quilts. Their elegance and precision never fail to inspire her. This is her first book, though she has published articles and projects dedicated to sewing for many years. She lives in Goshen, New York, with her daughter, husband, and dog.